T0113960

AWAKENING

9 Questions That Saved My Life

Mary Daniels

HAY HOUSE

Carlsbad, California • New York City
London • Sydney • New Delhi

Published in the United Kingdom by:
Hay House UK Ltd, The Sixth Floor, Watson House,
54 Baker Street, London W1U 7BU
Tel: +44 (0)20 3927 7290; Fax: +44 (0)20 3927 7291; www.hayhouse.co.uk

Published in the United States of America by:
Hay House Inc., PO Box 5100, Carlsbad, CA 92018-5100
Tel: (1) 760 431 7695 or (800) 654 5126; Fax: (1) 760 431 6948
or (800) 650 5115; www.hayhouse.com

Published in Australia by:
Hay House Australia Ltd, 18/36 Ralph St, Alexandria NSW 2015
Tel: (61) 2 9669 4299; Fax: (61) 2 9669 4144; www.hayhouse.com.au

Published in India by:
Hay House Publishers India, Muskaan Complex, Plot No.3, B-2,
Vasant Kunj, New Delhi 110 070
Tel: (91) 11 4176 1620; Fax: (91) 11 4176 1630; www.hayhouse.co.in

Text © Mary Daniels, 2015

The moral rights of the author have been asserted.

All rights reserved. No part of this book may be reproduced by any
mechanical, photographic or electronic process, or in the form of a
phonographic recording; nor may it be stored in a retrieval system, transmitted
or otherwise be copied for public or private use, other than for 'fair use'
as brief quotations embodied in articles and reviews, without prior written
permission of the publisher.

The information given in this book should not be treated as a substitute for
professional medical advice; always consult a medical practitioner. Any use
of information in this book is at the reader's discretion and risk. Neither the
author nor the publisher can be held responsible for any loss, claim or damage
arising out of the use, or misuse, of the suggestions made, the failure to take
medical advice or for any material on third party websites.

A catalogue record for this book is available from the British Library.

ISBN: 978-1-4019-6855-7

Interior images: 1, 57, 183 © Carmen Spitznagel/Trevillion Images
and Elisabeth Ansley/Trevillion Images

To all you beautiful souls out there going through your own Wild Awakening –
Hang in there, it's worth the ride!

Contents

Author's Note

I'm a strong believer in the idea that people come into our lives for a reason – to teach us things that will help us grow. And although it can sometimes be painful while we're in the thick of those lessons, afterwards it's amazing to see the gifts that this growth has offered us.

With this in mind, I've attempted to write this book with as much compassion and consideration as possible towards those mentioned in it – the people whose paths have crossed mine in such a powerful way. In exploring some of my deeper, more powerful lessons in this book, I've chosen to share some very raw and personal moments in my life that have involved family members, friends and past partners.

I've concealed the identity of these people as much as possible, but it's my hope that they can see the importance of sharing these lessons, and know that I in no way underestimate the depth of the feelings that may arise as a result. To them I say: I love you deeply and am eternally grateful for the role you have played in my growth and awareness of self. And I hope that others will also enjoy the opportunity for growth that our story offers.

Acknowledgements

My favourite page of the entire book: my thank yous!

To my son – aka living legend No.2 (you know who is No.1 ;-)
You have been my entertainment, my friend, my 360-degree
mirror, my teacher, my clinical trial for complementary medicine,
my financial pain in the arse – and at times my reason for living.
I am so proud of you, have often lived in fear of what you would
do next, and love you ;-) Seize life with both hands, son, for you
deserve it; remember that life only gives you what you put in.

To Mandena – my guardian angel, spirit guide and dearest friend
For your presence, guidance, lessons and being
among the pages of this book and throughout my life.
'Woman', you truly are a Gift from God, Consciousness
itself, no words are needed for this kind of love.

To the courageous men who dared to be in my life
Harry and Kwa – my heroes. Thank you for
just being you and being there!

My father – I love you, I chose you; rest in peace.

Daddy Slim – I love you and missed you all
my life. Thank you for picking me.

To Mr Ex – to our adventures, growth, love,
and your belief in this and me.

Cam – my surrogate 'girlfriend', best mate, and
proof that great men and fathers do exist!

'G' – the first man to really teach me about
self-love – you are so, so precious.

My adopted boys… love you and proud of you all.

Paul – for opening up your home and heart: you saved me!

And of course, Mr Italy – my 'perfect' mirror, equilibrium
and pain in the arse. Real Love, Mister!

To the powerful women who have inspired me and touched my life

My mum – I am so, so proud of you. I know this
journey was hard. For all that you are, I love you!

My foster mum – for being there for me whenever
I needed you, and for the love I always felt.

My sisters – for inspiring me and loving me
in such different ways; I love you all.

Kim – for all that you've given and all that
you deserved. I love you my dear.

My incredible sisters-in-law – your support has been a gift.

My sexy soul sisters – Anna (forever friends); Angie Pang (where
else, my dear) and Venetia (My Movie love); to Viv, my baby sis and
long-time champion and Michelle (my powerful little right arm) xx

Barbara, Vandana, Gill and Pauline –
Beautiful people, magical times!

Carole Catto – thank you for being there without
me even having to ask: you're an angel!

And to all the incredible WILD WOMEN in my life!!
You inspire me every single day! xx

Acknowledgements

A big shout out, hugs, massive snogs and gratitude to:
My big, crazy family: cousins, in-laws, Jack, Pat and Ish,
my Alternatives family and amazing volunteers!

The good people at St. James's Church in London, especially
Ashley and Revd. Lucy Winkett (Wise woman). My new Hay House
family, especially Michelle Pilley (The Wise Wild Woman that you
are; thank you so much for following your intuition; Jo for simply
being bloody marvellous! Leanne for the beautiful cover.
Julie Oughton for always making the dates work.
My phenomenal editor – Debra Wolter (there's good, and
then there's unbelievable!). The Holdens, Ruth and the rest
of the team: you guys rock!! Future Foundations – doing cool
things with young people! My Italian family at Tribewanted
Monestevole, Adrienne, Alison and The Mexican Exchange team!

And finally, to those I do not have enough space to list here: you
know who you are. Thank you for all the amazing life lessons; I am
so grateful to know you, love you and to have learned from you!

Introduction

I'm a Mess

I won't lie – when I was asked to write this book my initial reaction was: *Does the world really need another self-help book, and am I even qualified to write one?* Especially as in some ways, my life is still a mess.

I'd long thought that I'd love to write a book, and hopefully find a way to share my crazy experiences and powerful life lessons. But I struggled to think of a way of approaching it that wouldn't make it 'yet another self-help book'. I was tired of all those newspaper and magazine articles and blogs telling me what to do, how to live my life, how to think and be! '7 steps to this', '9 steps to that', '10 steps to eternal bliss and freedom!' I felt like shouting, *enough already!*

So you can imagine the dilemma I faced when Hay House, one of the world's largest spiritual and self-help publishers, asked me to join their amazing line-up of authors: especially as my story was a '9 Questions to…' journey. And there lies the irony of the situation, for in so many ways the space I thought I was becoming slightly disconnected from, was the same space that had actually helped me reconnect and find myself.

When I look over at my bookshelf and see the likes of *Into The Wild, A New Earth, Loving What Is, You Can Heal Your Life, True Meditation, Women Who Run With the Wolves, Confessions of an*

Economic Hit Man, Leaving Microsoft to Change the World and, most recently, *The One-Straw Revolution* and *Permaculture* by David Holmgren, it is hard to deny the impact these books have made and are still making in my life today.

I still can't believe that *Permaculture Magazine* – an environmental title that's all about self-reliance and sustainability – is now one of my most treasured magazine subscriptions. (A by-product of crossing a 6ft 6in – and rather cute – Italian permaculture designer with a burned-out city girl in the magical gardens of Monestevole in Italy: all will be revealed later, although calm yourself, ladies: this ain't no 50 Shades meets fruit and veg).

However, if it were not for the books, talks, workshops, events, incredible friends, teachers, work colleagues and Mandena (the most conscious person I know, and someone who has been my spiritual guide in ways I never saw coming), I honestly don't know where I would be, and how long it would have taken for me to translate all these intense and sometimes incredibly painful insights and experiences into something deeper and richer.

This is why I'm so excited about my mess – because in some warped and twisted way, it's showing me that I've never been happier, felt more secure in myself, or more trusting. For the first time after my very painful climb out of the really dark and deep hole called my life, I know and feel on every level that I am held and that life's got me.

Which is surprising because, at the same time, everything secure and safe is starting to fall away. My job, some of my closest friendships, my relationship, my home, my income, some family members: literally across the board. Well, everything except my flaming weight! (You'd think if God were going to clean the board, he would at least take a little bit of that with him too). Ah well... can't be too greedy!

But out of all of this, I've realized that in some ways, we are *all* a mess – every single one of us. From Eckhart Tolle and the Dalai Lama to the person we pass every day sleeping rough on the street.

No matter who we are, we all have our own mountain to climb, our own obstacles to overcome, our own lessons to learn: some that will continuously keep coming round to bite us on the backside.

And so this is why I have to keep things real. My story is not an overnight success or a life-changing transformation that happened at the click of my fingers. It took me years to discover the real answers to those simple yet powerful 9 Questions. It took me a long time to get my life 'on track' and really start liking and loving who I am, slowly feeling more and more comfortable in my own skin. You see my story is one of a real woman who thought she had it all, had read it all, heard it all and done it all, until she hit a wall.

This is a journey of a woman who was in so much pain, the idea of taking her own life and that of her child seemed to be the only way out. This is a tale of the raw, messy, magical and at times mind-blowing series of events that led me to discover 9 simple questions which, when answered in a certain way, opened doors I never would have imagined.

So as you delve into this largely uncensored, real, sometimes funny, other times downright stupid and exhausting path to self and 'sorting my life out', I hope you recognize that while my journey might have been a bit crazy and wild, I am no different to anyone else. I am not here to preach or to tell you how to live or be, and these 9 Questions alone are not going to fix every area of your life overnight – this is not a 'microwave your life to perfect' process and my Wild Awakening was not a lightning-bolt epiphany!

My hope in writing this book and sharing my story, is that I might inspire you to want to ask your own deeper questions about where you are at in your own life: how well it is working for you and what it is you really want. My hope is that it might inspire your own Wild Awakening, especially for those of you out there really suffering and in pain. My deepest hope is that this will become more than 'just another self-help book' that gathers dust on an overcrowded bookshelf.

My hope is that it will become a useful tool to help you find some much-needed answers to some much-needed questions: to help you navigate this crazy, amazing journey back to self – the one we call life!

How to get the most from this book

Just read it, and enjoy it! Honestly, just start at the beginning and keep going until you get to the end. If it doesn't make sense, re-read it – more slowly. And if it still doesn't make sense, then feel free to contact me directly via my website: www.marydaniels.co.uk

The book is organized into three parts:

Part I is my life story and it explains how a crazy, wild, raw, messy, magical and at times mind-blowing series of events led to an epiphany, and ultimately, the 9 Questions.

Part II reveals how I found the 9 Questions and explains how I've incorporated them into my daily life. Along the way it delves deeply into the powerful insights I've had while answering them, all interwoven with more of my juicy life experiences.

Part III shows you how to get started on your own Wild Awakening journey. It offers a simple guide to answering the 9 Questions and an overview of the other practices that have helped me along the way.

Part 1

The Wonder Years

Chapter 1

Another Day in Paradise

*'Life becomes precious and more special to us when
we look for the little everyday miracles and get excited
about the privileges of simply being human.'*
TIM HANSEL

Have you ever had a day, or even a moment, when everything was crystal clear and you were filled with such a sense of calm, and such unwavering clarity, that nothing or no one could knock you from that pillar? Well, that's exactly how I felt on the day I knew I was going to die. But we'll come to that part of my life later: first, here's the story of young Mary.

When I tune in to memories of my very early years, my body holds distant feelings of joy, playfulness, laughter and love. I was just a few weeks old when I was placed into foster care, along with my two-year-old brother. We joined a traditional working-class family of four – two parents, two kids – and my foster mum and Dad did what they could to make ends meet and raise their newly expanded family.

I was christened Mary, but my foster parents nicknamed me Missy because, as I grew older, I became bossy, outspoken, confident and very present. I'm told that I was well known to our neighbours, the local policemen and shopkeepers and the teachers at my brother's school. Apparently I could often be seen pushing my playmate Joseph – one of our cats – in my pram (I'd dress him up first – how the poor creature put up with that, God only knows!)

According to my foster mum, I was a chatty little mite, and when I wasn't in the garden, helping Dad with the veggies, I'd be talking away to our many furry friends – several cats, a chicken called Hilda, a cockerel called Danny, two dogs, two rabbits, two ducks (Susan and Thomas), and Joseph the donkey (we liked that name!). The latter had been rescued from a local field after Mum saw he was being maltreated. When the pets grew tired of me, I'd climb the makeshift ladder Dad had built on our fence, and chat to our next-door neighbour.

When I ask my foster mum about my personality in these early years, she says I was a law unto myself. I was a free, wild soul – always curious, always asking questions and always needing to know 'why'. Apparently I wanted to be a lawyer or an actress when I grew up: I've no idea where the actress idea came from, but the lawyer one must have resulted from my tendency to tell people what I thought, and to stop people being mean and bad. I'm still like this today!

My foster mum tells several funny stories about me that demonstrate how stubborn, or should I say strong-minded, I could be. On one occasion the Father from our church came to tea, and as we sat down, I announced that I couldn't wait for him to say grace before I started my food, because I was too hungry. He told me that I *must* wait – that it's important that we thank God for our food *before* we eat. But I was determined to tuck in: 'Why don't you say grace to the others, and I'll say mine when I'm done? I will be more grateful then!' I remarked. So, as the Father said grace, I sat munching loudly; afterwards, we had a special grace for Missy!

And when we dropped my brother off at his school each morning, I'd run around the playground as if I owned the place. One day the headmaster caught me running and playing on the grass. He called me over, pointed to a sign and said, 'Mary, what does that sign say?'

'It says: "Students, please keep off the grass," I replied. (Mum had taught me to read at a very young age.)

'That's right,' the headmaster continued. 'So why are you running on the grass, when it says not to?'

'Because I'm not a student!' I retorted, before running back onto the grass. The headmaster apparently then turned to my mum and told her he couldn't wait for me to start at the school! Sadly, though, that never happened.

Even now, I'm not entirely sure why or how things turned out the way they did – all I know is that one day home was with my foster family, and the next day it wasn't. I've been told different versions of the story about our return to our birth parents: some say that I went first and my brother followed later, after a few trial weekends. My brother says that when my dad went to pick him up in the car, he was told not to look back or to cry; one can only imagine what that must have felt like: he was only seven years old. I was only five myself, and have no memory of these events.

Chapter 2

The Wind Cries Mary

*'Every child deserves a champion, an adult who
will never give up on them, who understands
the power of connection, and insists that they
become the best that they can possibly be.'*

RITA PIERSON

When my brother and I returned to live with our birth parents, we joined our two younger siblings – our brother and sister – to make another family of six. But I felt this was a family I didn't know, and something in me sensed that things were never going to be the same again.

During the time with our foster family, I'd seen my birth parents only rarely: my brother and my foster mum say that, while we were in care, they visited us every now and then (there are photos of my first birthday party to confirm that), but it's no secret that there were plenty of last-minute cancellations and no-shows. My brother recalls that we spent a few weekends with them, but my mind is a blank on this.

I can't remember much about the period immediately following our return: most of what I have in my mind is feelings and a few fleeting memories – like snapshots in an album, frozen moments in time. But I do recall that it was a lot noisier and a lot more cramped in my new home; I remember standing by the kitchen sink and looking out of the patio doors at my brothers, who were riding their bikes round and round in circles on a small patch of concrete.

Until we moved to a bigger place a few years later, we were all squished into a tiny place in East London. The energy there was very different from that of my foster parent's house, with its big garden and furry friends. I can recall a feeling of wanting to go home.

Apparently, not long after rejoining the family, I started wetting the bed and eating the wallpaper off my bedroom wall. It's clear to me now that I was angry, sad and really lonely, but of course, at the time, I was far too young to know what to do with these emotions. Looking back on it, it's hardly surprising that I felt this way – after all, I'd been taken from the only family I'd known and placed in one that was full of strangers. But at the time my behaviour was regarded as 'naughty'.

The anger really came into play when I started at my new primary school. I'd roll around in the playground and beat up any boy who annoyed me, liked me or looked at me the wrong way. I also picked on a girl in my class; but then, one day, to my surprise, she did it back. I remember feeling respectful of her sparring ability, and her signal that she was a worthy opponent. Strangely, we became really good friends; I can still recall her tiny frame and sweet face!

By the time I was seven, my 'bad' behaviour had escalated, and my parents had resorted to using threats on a regular basis in a bid to control it, with my mother saying, 'Wait until your father gets home' and my father often saying, 'One day you'll be in hospital or dead, and I'll be in prison!' or 'Do you hear that? It's the sound of the police, and they're coming to take you away.'

For some reason it always felt as if my mum was at her wits' end with me; the jar of lollipops and sweets hidden in the cupboard would regularly be raided, and I'd cut tiny corners off material I could find – from the shower curtain to the tablecloth, and even a bed sheet – out of sheer boredom and curiosity. I only did it two or three times, but as you can imagine, it drove my parents crazy! Looking back now I can see that I had so much energy that I needed to be challenged and stimulated, constantly.

At the time, I didn't fully understand why I was always in so much trouble, and I just felt picked on. Having spoken to one of my brothers about this recently, I know that I wasn't the only one in the family who'd get into trouble or was beaten by our father. He has his own painful memories, and actually, thinking about it now, I even remember the odd physical fight between my parents. I never knew what started it but it was terrifying to see someone as big as my father swing punches at my mother; sometimes it would take a few of us to hold them apart.

However, I can see that for most of the time I existed inside my own bubble, my world totally taken up by the feeling of being unloved, and even unwanted. I remember, when I was about nine years old, purposely blaming one of my brothers for taking a £5 note from me. He hadn't done this – I had placed it in his shirt pocket and told my parents someone had taken it. I wanted them to stop seeing me as the bad one; I wanted them to realize I wasn't the only one who was being naughty.

What I didn't consider was what would happen to my brother as a result of my actions. I will never forget the look on his face after my dad had punished him. I hadn't intended to get him into trouble; I thought my parents would just tell him off, because in my mind they favoured him over me. The guilt of what I'd done stayed with me for years afterwards.

When my parents figured out what had really happened, boy did I pay for it. I remember going to bed that night and being unable to roll over because of the pain on my back and my bottom from the beating I'd received; I also had a splitting headache from a blow to the side of my head (it had hit a doorframe). I lay there thinking, *Serves you right, Mary – you deserve it for what you did to him*. I never tried anything like that again.

Meanwhile, the bedwetting continued – fuelled, I know now, by my constant state of fear and anxiety. My parents' reaction to this, especially my mother's, was rage and frustration: she complained that I was ruining the mattress, and on two occasions she actually held my head and rubbed my face in the mess. So, whenever I awoke in the night to find I'd wet the bed again, I was terrified of the consequences.

I'd get up and try to air my mattress, standing it on its side, next to the radiator. Then I'd quickly wash and dry my sheets, before opening the window to let out the urine smell. Or I'd put towels over the wet patch on the bed, before climbing back into it, hanging off the edge and pretending all was well under the duvet.

Every time I came home from school or elsewhere, adrenaline would flood my body as I put my key in the front door. I was constantly holding my breath, afraid of what the next yell of my name would bring. I'd try to stay out of the way, to avoid being a visual reminder of all the things I had or hadn't done. I would hide out in libraries, among my own books, and in any room in the house that felt 'safe'.

Basically, I'd do whatever it took to avoid the brunt of my parents' anger. My mother's was delivered in short bursts of frustration and disappointment – why couldn't I do the household chores she asked me to do properly? As for my father, I couldn't begin to tell you all the things that triggered his anger – but among them were breaking things and answering back. On one occasion, I'd done my hair in a particular style for church, and he told me that he didn't like it – that he never wanted to see that hairstyle on me again.

I remember thinking that if I didn't do my hair like that again for a couple of months, and then did it again – neater than the first time – he wouldn't mind. Well, that was the first and last time I ignored my father when it came to my hair. When we got home from church he dragged me by my hair into the back room, and after reprimanding me, he went to get a pair of scissors and then proceeded to hack off my hair. I was devastated: unlike my sister's hair, mine took a long time to grow. Everything had gone.

My mother was rarely violent, although I'd get the odd shove, slap or slipper across the back. However, I do remember the time she got so angry with me, she hurled an object at my head. It was a large, round, heavy ball of wax – a candle in the form of Mr Bump from the Mr Men – can you believe it! It hit me square on the forehead. Looking back on it, it seems ironic and even quite funny: under different circumstances I would have been impressed by my mum's throwing ability.

The pain above my eye was excruciating. Mum was visibly horrified by the sight of the swelling, which grew to the size of a tennis ball, and she sat me down and quickly applied a cold compress to it. She was clearly upset with me, and herself, and desperate to know why I couldn't just do as I was told.

In some ways it was worth the pain to see the genuine concern on her face; it was one of the few times when she showed me she cared. I can still remember how it felt to sit in that chair, almost touching my mum and not being scared of her; a part of me wanted to lean in and rest my cheek on her soft stomach, to take in deep breaths of her clean, sweet smell – cocoa butter and soap. I can still smell it now.

I learned only recently that Mum had struggled to control her anger during her menopause; at the time, of course, I had no idea of the role that might have played – I just believed that she didn't like me, even hated me at times.

My father's punishment methods, for things other than hairstyle rebellion, came in various forms, depending on the severity of the crime, or simply the type of day he'd had. He'd use a ruler or his hand – now and then administering a slap to the back or the side of the head. If you were really 'bad' you'd be whipped with one of his many canes – which were cleverly hidden behind doors – or his belt. He'd sometimes use the straightest object that came to hand, but most often he'd use his belt or a cane.

I was punished for taking food or sweets without asking; for occasionally breaking things; for not doing as I was told; or, simply bored with always being in trouble, for answering back, or saying things in the 'wrong' way (I didn't mean to do the latter, and it wasn't always my fault, but that rarely seemed to make a difference).

My most painful and shameful memories of being punished are around the times my father would make me take off part of my clothing, lie half-naked face down on the floor and keep completely still. As I held my breath, I would wait for him to announce the number of blows, knowing I would be silently counting my way through each searing contact of the belt or cane. I was forbidden to flinch or to make a sound as I was hit; if I did, my father would start all over again. I became good at getting lost in lands far away…

Afterwards, my father would try and get me to see the error of my ways; sometimes he even seemed shocked by his own loss of control – as if he was surprised at how violent he could become. I remember one particular incident that took place on a summer's day just before my tenth birthday; I've never forgotten it.

My father had come home from work in an angry mood, and on finding that the cat's food was missing, he yelled out from the kitchen: 'Who fed the cat?' We all responded that we hadn't. But then he came looking for me, asking the same question again and getting the same reply. He didn't believe me, and in a rage, he chased me down the hallway, hitting out and trying to grab me as he went. I was absolutely terrified; I remember running to the front door, shoeless, ready to open it and escape.

My heart was pounding and I knew I couldn't take another beating – not with that look in his eyes. As I stood there, with my hand on the cold chrome door latch, my father said, in a calm but determined voice, 'If you walk through that door you will never enter it again: that will be it.' And while I was so tempted to escape forever, the thought of wandering barefoot through the streets, looking for somewhere to stay for the night, terrified me even more than being beaten by my father.

Totally broken I let go of the handle, and followed him into the front room. I got undressed and lay half-naked on the floor, face down, and the lashes began. I tried to keep as still as I could, so he'd have to restart the count as few times as possible. After the tenth blow, I disappeared into one of the favourite places in my head.

Half an hour later, as I stood in the shower, my father came into the bathroom. On seeing the marks that covered the entire length of my back – and realizing that he'd just administered one of his worst punishments to date – he looked guiltier than usual. After placing a 50-pence piece on the side of the bath, he said the strangest thing: 'Sorry. But don't start thinking everything will be like the cat food.' I was unsure what he meant by that at first, but later I found out that none of us had fed the cat: its food was still sitting in the fridge and my father just hadn't seen it. Come to think of it, that was the last time he ever beat me like that.

—

Soon after I went up to secondary school, things started to take a very different turn at home. I'm not sure if I can say it was a turn for the worse or just a turn – all I know is that this second series of events involved a lot less physical pain than the first.

At school I was a year younger than many of my peers, due to my mid-August birthday, and was a bundle of contradictions: a bubbly, outwardly confident 'know-it-all' who was angry and full of anxiety. I was a sponge to my surroundings, trying to fit in anywhere and everywhere. I didn't have a clue who I was becoming, and what I was doing. I was so scared of not being liked, loved or accepted.

Dad now ended most of his evenings in the front room with a glass of something strong with ice; Mum would be in the back room, the second lounge as we called it, or in the dining room/kitchen. She'd be doing her own thing, often talking on the phone or cooking; they were both in their own worlds.

I'd become a bit of a hermit by then, finding solace in books. When it was time for lights out, I'd either pop on my little bedside lamp to read or study, or open the curtains and allow the street lamp to light the pages. I read ferociously, entering magical lands, harsh worlds and other people's lives – and my own life came alive among the pages.

The Brothers Grimm; *Flowers in the Attic*; autobiographies; Mills & Boon romances (I know, what can I say, I was searching for love!); Shakespeare's *Romeo and Juliet,* and *Antony and Cleopatra*, which my English teacher had brought to life so beautifully; Marlowe's *Doctor Faustus*; stories from the Old Testament; *Gulliver's Travels*; C.S. Lewis; Enid Blyton; Judy Bloom; *Of Mice and Men*; *A Streetcar named Desire*; *Cider with Rosie*. If there was a story that would transport me to another world, I devoured it. Books and studying were my sanctuary and my sanity.

I sometimes skipped meals, or went for long periods without eating. This was to avoid going into the kitchen and incurring Mum's wrath; she was often angry with me for not finishing a chore properly, or for being rude or disrespectful in ways I didn't understand. I was often told to stay away, to get out of her face, or a few other choice phrases that meant 'leave me alone'. So in defiance, sometimes I would do just that – knowing full well that meant no dinner.

As soon as I got home from school, I'd duck up to my room as quickly as possible, hiding out and waiting to see if Mum would call for me. Everyone thought my weight loss was down to an increase in exercise – and later on it was – but initially it was from missing so many meals. I will never forget the time my English teacher greeted me with the words, 'My goodness, Mary, it's like the fat ugly duckling has turned into a beautiful swan!' I'm sure she meant it as a compliment, but as I walked away I was thinking, *Oh my God: all this time she saw me as fat and ugly!*

Then, some time before my 11th birthday (I'm not completely sure when), came the day that changed everything. I remember arriving home from school to find that Mum was out, and quickly making my way to the kitchen to grab some food. I remember that I was still wearing my school uniform (I usually got changed out of it straight away, but on that day I needed to seize the opportunity to eat).

It's strange how one remembers the little things. I don't know why the memory of my uniform is so vivid. It wasn't particularly exciting – a grey polyester skirt with wide pleats that had been ironed so often you could see the shine on them, and a white polyester shirt that had gone grey and tired in the wash and stuck to me like a chemistry experiment on static electricity.

In our house, a step led into the kitchen, and my father was standing on that. I was standing next to the dining table. Seeing my face, he asked: 'What's wrong?'

I was surprised that he'd picked up on my mood – it wasn't like him to be so attentive. I wasn't in Mum's best books that week, and was feeling angry, upset and in dire need of attention, so I shared my frustrations with him, and my belief that my mother hated me. Still maintaining this concerned air, he spoke to me softly, assuring me that he would talk to Mum, get her to back off and give me space and time to study. I was shocked: who was this man?

'Come here,' he said, then, and not even hesitating to think about the path those small steps would take me on, I walked into my father's open arms and allowed him to engulf me in a hug that any little girl starved of love would crave (I'd never been hugged fully by either my father or my mother before this).

I had no idea that the soft caress of his hands, and the way he buried his head in the groove of my shoulder and pulled me in so tightly I could hardly breathe, was opening a forbidden door that he would find impossible to close again. And at that time I was blissfully unaware of the contract I had signed.

And then we both let out a sigh – but for very different reasons. I didn't know why my father was suddenly being so affectionate, and I didn't care – all I knew was that he finally loved me. And, sensing that this route would no longer bring me the physical and emotional scars of a belt, a whip or an object aimed in my direction, I unwittingly surrendered to the deal.

As my body changed and developed so did my father's interest in me. It progressed from hugging to getting me to undress in front of him, and finally to making me perform various sexual acts that seemed to keep him very happy.

I was learning very quickly that love and protection came at a price: the silent agreement of 'keep it up and I'll guarantee you peace and safety at home', was clearly understood. It seemed that my body was never to be my own, so I might as well utilize the offer on the table. Let's face it, for a child who had been through what I had, it seemed the lesser of the two evils.

When I look back I realize I'd be lying if I said that my childhood was all bad, or that I was being beaten all the time; it wasn't and I wasn't. In a strange way, while I didn't really feel loved, I knew on some level that my parents genuinely cared about me. As I've since learned, very few things in life are ever all one thing; I have repeatedly experienced that everything exists in one single moment.

So, as a child, I experienced many moments of happiness, unity, sharing, connection. Like the time we all crowded round our first TV set to watch Michael Jackson's video for the song *Thriller*, which had just come out. We later spent hours learning all the dance moves and how to make like a zombie. I also remember how, when we got our first VCR player, Mum would force us to record every biblical movie and TV show that was broadcast.

Books and music became my best friends. I remember the time my father came home with the most amazing Motown records from his then workplace. His music collection was incredible; we were not allowed to touch it, but when we had the occasional chance to listen to it, it was great!

I'll never forget the teasing I got when I bought my first album – Phil Collins's *Serious Hits Live*. I loved it. I think I was somewhere between 13 and 15 years old at the time, and I'd bought it with the money from my paper round. I played it on my first all-in-one moulded record player, which was designed to look like separate mixing decks. After that it was Elton John, and then – oh, my goodness – Michael Bolton. Okay, that one *was* a step too far, and it earned me the nickname 'bounty bar' (black on the outside, white on the inside), but I didn't care – I liked those artists and I *loved* music; after books, music kept me alive.

My favourite time of year was Christmas. Dad would play Bing Crosby's 'White Christmas', which was our cue to jump out of bed and rush excitedly downstairs, as if there were presents waiting for us under the tree – there weren't! Our gift was a stocking in the shape of a netted boot, stuffed with chocolate bars, which we found at the end of our beds on Christmas morning. One year Dad forgot to buy these, and so he told us they had been given to the starving children in Africa.

I remember feeling proud and happy about that: knowing that somewhere a hungry child was munching away on my Mars bar (ha ha, yes I know!) But I was also the girl who was devastated – at the age of 14 – to discover there was no Father Christmas. I still remember how upset I was!

Mum used to say I was the only one who really 'did' presents. I remember saving up for weeks before Christmas, and writing a list of the gifts I was going to buy – things for one or two friends and for everyone in my family. I would be lying if I said my gifts were creative: they were a handful of toiletries, a pair of socks or little knick-knacks.

I remember one year wrapping up a pile of one-penny sweets so my younger brother would think he had loads of gifts to open; or sometimes I'd wrap things in odd-shaped boxes to disguise them.

I loved giving presents and I loved watching people's excited faces as they unwrapped them; I learned that the pleasure lies more in the unwrapping than the gift itself. I actually think I was more excited about my gifts than the recipients were.

What can I say though? I loved Christmas, and thinking about it now, I can see why. Christmas was about Mum cooking the beast of a turkey Dad brought home every year from work; it was about my parents going to numerous church functions and gatherings; and Mum in particular spending hours watching biblical films and TV shows: all of which meant that we kids were basically left in peace. And also, overall, Christmas was the one time of the year I really felt we experienced what gratitude and abundance truly meant.

When our parents went out, my siblings and I would play the silliest games. We'd dress up and role-play, and have all-night Monopoly marathons. These would often bring out my competitive streak – the winner was usually the player who could buy up the most property, and stay awake the longest.

We were also quite a funny, witty bunch – sarcastically tearing chunks out of each other with our words and constantly teasing. My wicked sense of humour was often satisfied. One day, to my surprise, Mum pointed out that I was the only one in the family who really knew how to take a joke as well as give it out. My brothers and sisters may still beg to differ, but I was more shocked that Mum had noticed this, and her observation has stayed with me to this day.

Chapter 3
Fix You

*'A strong woman knows she has strength enough
for the journey; but a woman of strength knows...
it is in the journey where she will become strong.'*
UNKNOWN

Between the ages of 13 and 15, I became a fast learner when it came to keeping my father happy with sexual acts. And the happier he was, the happier we all were. As time went on, he became possessive and jealous with me. He'd go through my belongings, looking for notes and love letters from boys, and if he found any he'd either destroy them or demand to know what I was 'giving them' in return for such loving words. I insisted I'd given them nothing, that we just talked, but he didn't believe me.

Then, some time after I turned 15 or 16, what little tenderness my father had shown me started to go, and he sometimes left me bruised and sore. I was always acutely aware of his whereabouts in the house, and I was constantly managing the delicate balance between avoiding him and giving in to his requests. I knew I needed to do just enough to keep me safe and out of trouble, relishing the fact that his belt or worse hadn't been raised towards me in anger for a long time.

But the pulling, grabbing, pinching, shoving his and my hands wherever he liked was becoming tiring. Sometimes after our encounters he'd get me to sit over a bucket of hot water, believing it was a form of contraception; or he'd leave a small note of 'apology' for the way he had been – both of which made me feel cheap and dirty.

Now and then, to ease his conscience and keep me quiet when he'd been particularly heavy-handed or ignored my obvious upset, he would resort to leaving money next to my body when he was done, often throwing it down. I was starting to feel like his child whore; I belonged to him and to him alone.

By the time I was 16 I'd come to the conclusion that my mother loved me only when I was good and did as I was told, but the problem was I didn't always know what 'good' looked like, nor did I remember half the stuff I was told. As for my father, it was in his interest that my relationship with my mother remained difficult – after all, he couldn't offer protection if there was nothing to protect me from.

~

Meanwhile, at school, just as I did at home, I wore several masks. Over the course of my education, I attended four schools. After primary school came a local state school where, during the first year, my defiant behaviour towards one teacher in particular became a problem. I felt he was unsuited to teaching, as he couldn't engage with the children, teach them properly, or hold the attention of a class.

One day, during one of his lessons, he addressed some comments to me that I felt were uncalled for, so I walked out. Frustrated, he followed me. Things escalated and he eventually lost his rag, grabbed my throat, and started strangling me outside the school gates. Needless to say, my father removed me from that school and I think, out of sheer desperation to give his 'exceptionally bright but challenging' daughter a good education, he enrolled me in a private Catholic convent school.

I wasn't sure what was worse: the fact that it was a convent school, or that it was girls only. In fact, before I started there, my parents didn't tell me about the all-girls part, and – ridiculously – it took me two weeks to work it out. I kept thinking that the boys were going to join us later! I must have been in shock!

At 17 I was back in a local mixed grammar school. I was determined to enjoy this new environment, so I got stuck in. I helped run the junior basketball team, and I sometimes played football, joking around with the boys during breaks. To my surprise, I was nominated for head girl and ended up becoming deputy head girl, ahead of many candidates who had been at the school for years.

I also became involved in fund-raising events, wrote and delivered some of the school assemblies, and became good friends with a couple of the teachers – on more than one occasion I sat with them in the staff room, quietly enjoying the banter as they shared their true thoughts around their day and life in general.

I was starting to learn I could integrate well, and that I was a survivor. I raised funds for myself through multiple paper rounds, and a small Maths and English tutoring business I'd started up. I was earning enough money to cover my meals, pay for my school books, buy new clothes – and for the first time, I could go out clubbing (not that I did, much). But I was free and happy. And I'd found my first true best friend – a bond that's still going strong today.

—

Then came the summer of change. When I was 17, our church invited me on a youth exchange visit to Mexico. Surprisingly, my parents agreed to let me go – anything related to the church usually got the thumbs up. But none of us knew that this trip would play a major part in turning the situation at home on its head. It was the first time I'd ever properly been away from home – and my first time on a plane. I was finally free, without my father watching my every move and pouncing at will. I felt as if I'd entered a parallel universe.

I was the youngest in the group and initially I found it hard to be with everyone (despite outward appearances I'm actually quite shy). We moved around constantly during the trip, staying with the different families in the exchange group, and I loved it. I got to experience what it was like to be a part of a Mexican family – witnessing their lifestyle, their community, their culture, and seeing their openness and love of life.

It was beautiful to be a part of it: to see generosity, love and support between communities who didn't always have a lot – materially – really opened my eyes to what matters in life. Ironically, it took a trip across the ocean to finally see what 'normal' and 'love' looked like. The team in Mexico were great, and the bond between the two groups was evident. I left moved by what I'd seen, and certain that I no longer wanted the life I had, or to continue in the role my father had forced me to play.

When we arrived back in the UK, I was upset to find I was the only one who didn't have anyone to meet them at the airport; in hindsight, it shouldn't have surprised me, as I'd also been the only one who hadn't received a letter the entire time we were in Mexico. Anyway, after gratefully accepting the offer of a lift from a dear friend's mum, I returned home, determined to turn over a new leaf.

So when I met my mum and saw that she'd actually missed me – and was eager to try and bridge the gap between us – you can imagine how shocked I was! I will never forget the time she asked me to sit on her lap, so she could try and tell me how much she loved me. Even though it was the most non-flowing, awkward moment we'd ever shared, I could feel her genuineness, her desire to try and connect.

I wasn't certain of the source of this turnaround in her behaviour, but what I did know was that I wanted it to stay, and that I was going to work hard to hold on to it. (Of course, she was still upset that, before I left, I hadn't decanted a tin of tomatoes into the correct Tupperware container! To this day I still laugh about this – that was Mum).

So, the following day, when my father called me into his bedroom to talk, I was ready for him: my speech rehearsed and my spirits high. I launched into it, excited about the fresh start, the new possibilities, and the opportunity finally to experience family life the way it should be – the way I'd experienced it on my trip.

But it wasn't long before I could see we were on two very different pages; my father's eyes held the longing of someone who'd been starved; someone who'd had to wait a whole summer for that thing he could so readily take right now. I knew my words were falling on deaf ears. Mum was out and I think the rest of the family were dotted around the house, lost in their own worlds. Desperate for him to show me that his love extended further than me meeting his physical needs, I tried to appeal to his softer side.

'Dad, I don't want to do this any more…nothing needs to change; I promise I won't tell anyone. I just want us to be normal and for this to stop.'

Nothing – just laughter and a deepening of his hungry, knowing smile.

'Dad…' I pleaded, trying to connect with him over the laughter. Then I got up to leave, seeing it was pointless. He pulled me back down next to him, and said: 'When you leave home we'll stop, but not now; I've missed you.'

'Dad, stop it – listen, can't we just talk? We don't have to do this.'

Rolling me backwards, he leaned over me, his full weight on my left side, quietly chuckling as he pulled his knee up between my thighs.

'Dad,' I half shouted, pushing upwards as his grip became firmer and stronger. I was hoping he wouldn't pick up on my panic and my mental fears about where next I should take this conversation.

'Dad, please: don't do this,' I went on, determined not to let him see my tears. The words rolled off my tongue and onto the floor, where they lay, looking up at me, lost and helpless. He parted my legs wider, crushing me under the weight of his solid trunk. Determined to go for it one last time, I forcefully said, 'If you don't stop right now, I will scream.'

He paused, his heavy breath warming my earlobe. *It's worked*, I thought. *I have his attention – he does care!* Slowly, he lifted his head, looked me straight in the eye and coolly said, 'No, you won't.'

And then I knew the fight was over. Of course I wouldn't: we both knew that. I had been far too well programmed over the years. What would happen to me if someone walked in now? I knew the drill; I was the liar, the troublemaker, remember. No one would believe me over him. He was my protector, until he wasn't. My newly forged bond with my mother was still too recent for me to trust it fully.

And finally, as I well knew, God had made me for this purpose: to make my father happy and keep the family together. And God doesn't make mistakes and things happen for a reason. I'd been told all of this since the tender age of 10 or 11. He had done well, and we both knew I wouldn't scream. He had won.

As I let the tears quietly fall, I left my body and watched from above as he used the force of his 6ft 2in muscular frame, and the give of the springs on the bed, to lift my skirt and open my shirt. I could feel his arms sweep up the side of me, in one smooth movement, pinning my wrists under his wide flat palms and pressing them firmly into the knotted white cotton throw.

Then I felt the knuckles of his fist press against my stomach as he released the zipper on his grey, worn-out polyester trousers. But none of this mattered: Mary had long gone; with every move he made, I was floating higher and higher – soaring, dancing free amongst the clouds. Protected, out of sight.

I struggle to use the word 'rape' to describe this incident, because my father had been 'taking what he wanted' for years, in return for 'protection' from my mother and some twisted form of love. But on this occasion I hoped he would pass the 'test' I'd set him: to listen to what I was saying about not wanting this to continue, and to stop when I asked him to. I prayed that he would pass this test, as it would show me he cared and that he would never do anything that purposely hurt me. Looking back, I can see that I needed to know if he really loved me or just loved *this*.

As it slowly came to an end, I looked down at the vacant face of a newly hopeful 18-year-old girl, and I realized it was time to accept that the father I thought I knew – the one I believed had loved me all this time – didn't exist. As he rolled away from me and cleaned himself off, there were two things I was certain of in that moment. Firstly, that this was the last time I'd ever look to him for love, and secondly, that he would never lay a finger on me again.

Chapter 4

Lucy in the Sky with Diamonds

'We cannot teach people anything; we can only help them discover it within themselves.'
GALILEO GALILEI

I've learned to assume that in every moment we're being asked to show up as both a teacher and a student, because we never know when we might meet the person who has something really powerful to teach us about ourselves and our life – and it's likely that we'll never really recognize that moment until it's passed.

In the same way, we don't always know when something we've said or done has really inspired or helped another person. So with that in mind, I've learned that it's far safer to try and live as if every encounter and every moment is asking me to step up as both a teacher and a student at the same time.

I feel very lucky to have had some powerful teachers/mentors throughout my life, and while I didn't always realize it at the time, looking back I can see they've always been there. Later in the book, you'll get to meet my dear friend, spiritual guide and mentor, Mandena – she's definitely something special. A conversation with her is like talking to pure consciousness; it's like a mirror into the heart of my soul – the most honest part of myself. She's always questioning me, pushing me and getting me to look at what's going on behind my thoughts, actions and emotions.

And back when I was around 17 years old, I met my first spiritual teacher. I guess he was around 20 years my senior, an ex-Hare Krishna, and someone I can only describe as strangely addictive – in a weird, almost messed-up, but together kind of way. As a way of protecting his identity, I'll call him Mr Stoner Zen!

I was introduced to him through a friend, and we pretty much hit it off straight away. I remember our first trip out together – it was to his favourite bookstore in London, an esoteric gem called Watkins, just off Charing Cross Road. It was like entering something from a Harry Potter story: the kind of store you would find on Diagon Alley (I loved those books). The smells, the colours, the magic and charm of the place; it was a real treasure trove – a sensory delight of East meets West.

Little did I know that several years later, my role as co-director of mind-body-spirit organization Alternatives would involve me getting to know and work closely with the team at the bookshop. It's funny the way life quietly reveals its well-designed path: like little breadcrumbs. Looking back, I can see how many of my greatest life lessons have come from the men in my life – which isn't surprising when I think about the dynamic between myself and my father, and my soul's journey with the masculine.

And at this point in my life, the lessons were coming from Mr Stoner Zen. He was excited by my eagerness to learn and grow, and I loved his eagerness to teach me. We couldn't get enough of our respective roles, entering into what I can only describe as a bizarre contract.

My mind and my senses were alive and being exposed to so many things I never knew existed: Ken Wilbur, Zen Buddhism, meditation, mindfulness… I was waking up to a whole new world – one that was full of infinite possibilities and higher consciousness; it was a new way of thinking and being.

I was also waking up to the fact that I'd totally fallen for Mr Stoner Zen; some would say it was more of a crush, but I'd already had many of those. This felt like a full mind, body, soul immersion, something I've realized I come to do a lot with the male teachers in my life. Sometimes, as Mandena has said, it's the only way life can get me to be still enough to hear and understand the messages it's sending me!

By this time, life at home had become a war zone. My father was constantly on edge, and very wary of this newfound confidence I was connecting to. I'd started answering him back and challenging him with knowing eyes, fully aware he no longer had a hold on me; I didn't care. Until one day in the kitchen, after one of our many catty altercations, he snapped, and before I knew it, his hands were around my throat.

There was such rage and despair in his eyes as his fingers started to press down, harder and harder. He was desperate to put an end to his fairytale gone wrong. I remember looking him square in the eyes and thinking, *Go on, do it: I dare you. Keep going. What can you take from me that you haven't already?* Suddenly aware that he was almost strangling his daughter, he let go. He knew he'd lost his little girl and it scared him.

⏤

So Mr Stoner Zen's flat became my place of escape, my sanctuary. We'd cook and chat, and now and then we'd get stoned. I'd never tried cannabis before we met, and was hypersensitive to stimulants: I didn't smoke, didn't drink, and would get ridiculously giggly and light-headed just sitting in a room full of people puffing away. So initially he was wary about letting me try some of his infamous, cannabis-laced chilli con carne.

I will never forget the first time I got stoned. Mr Stoner Zen locked me in his flat, fearful of finding me wandering around the streets, half-naked. Once I reached the dizzy heights of infinity and beyond, he blasted the space with the powerful sounds of peace, pain and rock and roll – from Hendrix to Nick Drake, Joni Mitchell to Bob Dylan, along with regular intervals of Prince.

We lay back, absorbed the vibrations and got lost in the universe! It was mind- blowing and afterwards it took me a couple of days to float back down to Earth. But, as much as we had a blast getting stoned, looking back I'm relieved that it didn't become an 'addiction', on top of everything else going on in my life

At the time my best friend was the only person who really knew what was going on between me and Mr Stoner Zen, and for obvious reasons she neither liked nor trusted this odd pairing. From the outside it looked like 'older, pervy man takes advantage of young, vulnerable girl', especially since she was aware that he knew about my dad. But from the inside it felt magical, special; I was learning so much. In fact we both were: about each other, about ourselves and about the wonder of life. It was impossible to stop – a soul contract that needed to run its course.

Stoner Zen initially found it amusing to challenge my religious beliefs. I talked about Jesus as if he were my best friend – someone I spoke to every day – and to be honest his presence *was* that for me back then. In the times I'd felt alone or abandoned as a child, my quiet conversations with him kept me going, and kept me hoping there was something better out there; something bigger waiting for me.

However, Zen saw me as a deluded Sunday worshipper: someone who had been taught how to be a Christian but hadn't really understood or experienced what it really meant – just words in a book, lectures from sermons. So we talked about the wider spiritual definitions of God; how some people call it their intuition, inner voice, life, the Universe, consciousness, being present, bliss, even nature.

I remember thinking, *Oh my goodness – there are so many different ways to connect to the same thing*. He also taught me what it means to be truly present – to live every moment as if it were your last – and why worrying is pointless. He taught me about the spiritual side of religion – how we are apparently timeless and ageless beings.

If I'm honest, it was a lot for me to take in at that age, and while I understood most of it as concepts, much of it stayed in my head, going round and round, expanding my mind. Now and then I'd feel something moving within me, like a little Mary quietly knocking on my internal doors and gently whispering, *Wake up, sleepy head!*

At the time, I had no idea of the extent of the seeds that were being planted, and how they would soon blossom into a wild garden, and later a little orchard that would eventually recognize itself in a tiny vegetable garden on top of a mountain in Italy. But until then, they settled down, patiently waiting for the right time.

As well as enjoying our deep conversations on enlightenment and what it meant to 'be', Mr Stoner Zen was fascinated by my apparent ability to 'read him' so quickly and accurately. He loved to ask me randomly to 'read' one of his friends, too: to tell him, on the spot, what sort of person they were, any fears I could feel from them, what they thought about themselves and how the world perceived them.

It was almost like a party trick, and he'd clap his hands as people nodded their heads in recognition as I spoke. I had no idea how it worked, or even why it was such a big deal, but he seemed to get immense mileage from it, often sitting in a chair adjacent to me and asking me to tell him what I saw. To be honest, he did love himself!

On reflection, I can see that this intuitive side of me had developed over the course of my early years as a form of protection – a survival mechanism as I learned how to read and interpret the treacherous waters at home. Over time I've learned we all have the ability to tune in to what's going on, not only inside us but with those around us. It's just that a lot of the time our external environment and mind chatter are so noisy and busy, they drown out any 'real' or subtle messages.

What I also learned, and have experienced in a very powerful way since, is that we are wonderful, amazing balls of energy – we're almost like mini croutons in a big bowl of soup, in that each of us, as human beings, are the croutons and the soup is the energy field we're all connected to, feeding off each other's 'vibes'.

However, because the soup is clear, invisible to the naked eye, we don't believe it's there, so many of us are floating around believing we exist as little crouton 'islands', completely separate and disconnected from each other and only paired when we meet 'the one' or our 'soulmate' – a term that's generally misunderstood, and sometimes turns into the 'ball and chain' or 'him/her indoors'!

Anyway, I soon found out that spiritual teachers, or any teachers come to think of it, are human beings with their own challenges, flaws and demons to face. I will never forget when my own mentor, Mandena, warned me of this: 'Mary, just because you are learning so much, don't put me or others on a pedestal. I have my own blocks, challenges and hurdles to overcome.' Looking back I can see how I was doing that all the time with Mr Stoner Zen.

In the meantime, though, we talked, went clubbing and experimented with a small selection of his array of hallucinogenic drugs (this was always done under strict supervision, as the tiniest dosage could spin me out of control; I was continuously shocked at how hypersensitive I was). I remember going to a couple of parties with him that definitely expanded my awareness of how people express themselves. On some occasions I felt slightly out of my depth, despite pretending that I was comfortable and confident in that space.

I'll never forget the first time I went to one of them – it was an Erotica party, and the dress code was leather and PVC. I remember sipping on a glass of lemonade while trying to have a serious conversation about life and career paths with an ex-accountant who was covered from head to toe in a black PVC catsuit, decorated with a silver studded dog collar and a long metal chain. He insisted on staying on his hands and knees throughout the conversation, despite there being an empty chair next to me, and at the end he asked me if I would like to 'take him for a walk' to the 'back rooms'.

Trying not to choke on my drink I sweetly declined his offer, saying I was waiting for some friends. Also, I'd already briefly had a wander through those back rooms, curious to see the mysteries they held, and had caught a glimpse of people stripping for their partners, beds with videos, cages with toys, and eventually, individual rooms with big round windows for all to see and anyone to join in.

Now, while I like to believe I'm quite open-minded, I did find these parties quite an eye-opener at the time. But after a while I saw that people went to them for very different reasons: it might be for some form of release, an exploration and expression of self, almost an escape from their mundane lives. Like a fancy-dress party that allows you to come as any version of your self that your heart secretly desires.

However, for others it was a lot darker – almost an unhealthy suppression – and despite my naivety I sensed that and preferred to hang out in the well-lit front rooms with familiar faces, a normal dance floor and bar – well, as normal as can be expected under the circumstances – carefully dodging the men who'd approach me with an invitation in their eyes, curiously drawn to the newcomer who was clearly 'fresh on the scene' and 'innocent'.

~

I can see now that at this time I had huge blinkers around how I saw myself physically: I had a well-toned, hourglass figure and quite striking facial features, yet I was convinced I was undesirable. When I look back on a couple of modelling photos I once did for a friend as a favour, I can't believe I ever doubted myself.

I would continually discount any possibility that a man might want anything more from me than friendship, and I walked away in the middle of several attempts by men to try and muster up the courage to ask me out, or even share their undying love. Convinced they were being silly, I'd sometimes argue with them, telling them they didn't know what they were talking about! Those poor men...

And over the course of my life my 'blind spot' – and my inability to read this side of some men – led to a few very close calls with men who thought that something else was 'on offer' and when it wasn't, they decided to try and 'take it'.

After Mr Stoner Zen and I had known each other for just under a year, our relationship started to take a different turn. Until that point we hadn't really been properly intimate – we'd cuddled and massaged each other, and done everything else but 'it'. But for some reason, despite my eagerness to please, he fought hard to hold back. But one night, as one of our chilli sessions culminated in him watching me, rather bemused, as I sat with my face pressed up against the TV screen, engrossed in the movie *Barbarella*, the inevitable happened.

Afterwards, suddenly realizing the possible consequences of our unplanned and unprotected actions, he panicked, running off to the bathroom, to 'see what he could find'. I followed him there, and found him stood next to a bucket of boiling water. He assured me that sitting over it would help. In shock, I quietly squatted over the bucket, unable to believe what was happening; I said nothing, but my insides were shaking, every cell in my body too terrified to voice the obvious feeling of déjà vu. The only difference being that the last man who'd asked me to do this was my father.

Looking back I can see how stupid and naive I was – despite everything that had happened with my father, it had not crossed my mind to sort out some form of birth control. But why would it? I'd never had a boyfriend – I didn't think anyone would be interested in me – and no one had sat me down and shown me my options.

Anyway, despite all the warning bells, I had fallen hard for Mr Zen; I think part of the attraction was his wildness – he had no real boundaries, and always liked to push the status quo. Sometimes this was for other people's growth, but occasionally it was for his own gain and pleasure, often with little regard to the devastating ripple effects it would have on those around him.

I'd confided in him about my dad and I could see he wanted me to leave home as soon as possible; but in reality this often became a forgotten subject. That is, until things got out of hand at home, and Zen finally convinced me to talk to a trusted teacher in my school. I eventually agreed and I have to say I'm eternally grateful to that teacher – not only did he listen to me, he also offered me a safe place, inviting me to stay with him and his wife.

After we'd slept together, every encounter with Mr Stoner Zen started to feel more and more intense, and I became totally lost in our own little bubble. However, it had to burst at some point, and that's exactly what happened. Out of the blue he turned up one day with a new 'friend' he'd started dating, thinking it would be nice for us to meet.

Initially, I tried to act all grown-up, swallowing the feeling that I'd been tossed aside like a toy he'd suddenly grown tired of. I made an effort to get to know her – she was nice and hadn't done anything wrong – but I could no longer sit on the sidelines, allowing myself to be pulled out to entertain him at his will.

So in pain, and feeling terribly rejected, I said 'yes' to the next man who showed me any real attention – grateful for the potential security and love he could offer. He was more than 16 years my senior, and this 'yes' turned into an 18-year rollercoaster to hell and back. And while he was not a bad person, as you'll see in the next chapter, he was definitely one of my greatest teachers on how *not* to love yourself. Sadly, this Wild Awakening was one I failed to learn for a very long time, with each round becoming more and more painful and intense.

Chapter 5

Both Sides Now

*'To understand your fear is the
beginning of really seeing.'*
BRUCE LEE

Fear is a funny thing: it can make us do things that, ordinarily, we'd never do. Sometimes we're unconscious of the depth of our fears, and how much they are influencing our decision-making process.

Strangely, this chapter about my ex-partner has been the hardest one to write, although I'd no idea that this would be the case when I started. In my first draft, I could see I was still angry/bitter about a few things that had happened between us, and then, second time around, I became over-protective, worried about what his new partner and his kids might think, or his family – in particular, his father, who has been a great friend and champion of mine and has no idea of what went on between us.

So that's why this relationship, out of all the ones I've had, has been the hardest to write about, simply because I know that the man behind the behaviour adored me at the time we were together. He has a very good and generous heart – something his friends and family would all agree on – but I also know that our relationship was, in many ways, the most damaging relationship I've had in my life to date.

Without going into too much detail, as that will serve no real purpose, I can honestly say it destroyed my confidence, my self-belief, my sense of worth, and it sucked the small amount of self-love I had right out of me – something I'm still recovering from, in many areas of my life.

~

The first time I properly met Mr Ex, as I shall call him, I was 19 and he was 35. I was working in his and his then wife's business. At the end of one working day, I was busy washing the dishes in the kitchen – clearing up the lunch plates before going home – when Mr Ex came in to fix the *supposedly* broken fridge.

At the time I was feeling down because Mr Stoner Zen and I were becoming so distant, and this had made me feel so rejected. Although I was lost in my thoughts as I washed the dishes, I remember Mr Ex standing at the fridge for ages, trying to engage me in conversation. Eventually it worked, and we chatted for hours. Later on, he confessed there had been nothing wrong with the fridge!

There was an instant charge between us; it was so strong that every time I passed him in the hallway it was as if an electric current had ran through me. I had never felt that before and it was overwhelming. A few weeks later, he invited me to a large business conference – as a businessman he was always looking at the next 'big thing'. During our kitchen chat I had spoken about my dream of running a business, and he thought my personality would fit in perfectly with his new business project.

In my usual chaotic style, I turned up late for the event and missed it. Feeling awful, and concerned that I'd made him waste money on a ticket, I went round to his home to apologize. As I mentioned, at the time he was married, and he had children, and although it was rumoured that all was not well in the relationship, it wasn't something we'd discussed.

When I arrived he said his family were away for the weekend, but that I was welcome to stay for dinner. If I'd known then what I do now, I would have turned around and kept walking, but at the time I remember thinking, how sweet! As we chatted, I sat there, nervously looking at the clock, mindful that I was a penniless student with a return train ticket that was about to run out. But I was enjoying the conversation, so I threw caution to the wind and decided to go with the moment.

I was completely unaware that he had something else on his mind; something that took me a while to figure out – not just then, but later in life, with other men too. It's easily done when you've been taught, and believe, you're completely undesirable.

Before I knew it, I was having an affair. We didn't meet often and I wasn't working out a strategy for catching him; in fact, I had no game plan and NO idea what was happening. I felt awful for his then wife, and I felt ashamed of myself – I never thought I'd be anyone's woman, let alone the 'other one', and in one sense I didn't even see myself as that.

We were fulfilling unspoken roles. I just liked the fact that someone liked me: it made me feel wanted. Plus, I felt guilty that I'd gone this far; I couldn't suddenly drop him as I didn't want to hurt him. It was that sad and that simple. I'd gone from having to guess whether I was even lovable to feeling as if I was the centre of someone's universe. And living in Holland!

Hold up, Mary! Holland? How did that happen?

Well, to cut a long story short, after I'd left school things hadn't quite gone to plan. I'd messed up my A levels, due to inconveniently falling in love with Stoner Zen, and had ended up at a university that hadn't been my choice, studying a course I never really got into. I still wanted to learn something, but I was also desperate to travel, and to start a business, as I was in need of money.

At that time Mr Ex was writing to me regularly about his travels – about his new business in Holland – and his growing love for me. Mistaking the security and adventure that he offered for being head over heels in love, I started to miss him terribly. After he promised to take me with him to Holland once he'd become more settled there, I decided I was going to work out a plan to start my own business – to continue my studies while going to Holland to be with my new 'love'.

So, with pen and paper in hand I mapped out my 'what next'. (I remember someone once asking me, 'Why didn't you just get a job?' If I'm honest, the thought didn't even cross my mind, even though that would have been the normal thing to do. However, my life has shown me that I tend to walk anything but the normal path.)

At college my main lectures fell on a Monday and Tuesday, so I managed to get someone to cover my single Wednesday lecture and then I was off, starting what was to become the beginning of an exciting new chapter in my life. Initially, I commuted back and forth to Holland, but roughly six months later, I'd moved out there.

I loved it all: the people, the place, the excitement of building something from scratch, and actually getting to know a different side to Mr Ex. Plus, I found it was slightly easier to suppress the shame and guilt of being the 'other' woman from a different country.

I'm not sure whether I was naturally good at business, or whether everyone I worked with was just so surprised I was just 19 years old: either way, things started to go well. Looking back on the business we were doing, I can see it was a typical network marketing model – sell the dream and nothing else. But at the time I'd never come across network marketing, so I genuinely believed that, with my environmental products (commercial and personal air-filtration systems and carbon water-purifiers) in tow, I was going to save people from toxic air and poisoned drinking water.

As a sideline I was also going to teach people who were struggling financially how to earn an additional income, to grow their own business; and at the same time I'd make loads of money, get to travel and become rich! God, I was naive – and slightly dazzled by the whole thing. But making money wasn't my main driving force: being free, happy and loved were. So I went to work with my naivety and belief in what I was doing, and they really served me well.

—

Initially, with a lot of help and support from Mr Ex, I started to learn the ropes; I made some sales and started running presentations. I moved in with Mr Ex and his flatmate, had my own little network and enjoyed seeing Mr Ex in full business flow as a determined, hard-working salesman and entrepreneur. It's something I've always admired about him – his work ethic and his determination to see a project through; in fact, it's something we both loved and respected about each other.

Now *my* business creativity took a different form: I loved people – seemed to draw them to me – and my big-vision thinking and lack of boundaries or awareness of personal safety brought me different kinds of adventure. With Mr Ex having to spend more time in the UK, and with his family, I was forced to think up ways to partner with local businesses. I came up with the idea of printing off some business cards from a machine in the local train station; these were so flimsy and cheap, you could almost see through them!

I thought I'd add something intriguing to them: to grab people's attention. Well, as I write this now, I can't stop laughing about *those* business cards: on one side were my contact details and on the other was the following: 'I have something I think you would really be interested in: call me if you are curious to discuss further.'

Deciding that people with expensive cars would have money to invest in my business, I proceeded to walk the streets of Eindhoven and hang out in airport car parks, placing the cards under the windscreen wipers of the vehicles of regular overseas commuters (remember: there was no internet in those days!).

Anyway, my determination won me many appointments, a couple of strong business partners and a call from a man who owned a bright red Ferrari. He wanted to meet, and as far as I was concerned, if someone so obviously successful was interested in me, I was on my way! Excitedly, I put together the best presentation pack I could manage.

At the meeting, I pulled out my sample air and water filter, and showed him my plastic hole-punched ring binder display, full of stats on air quality and pollutants in water. The Ferrari owner sat positioned behind a huge long table, and two big strong burly men in black suits stood either side of me. He didn't say a word during my presentation, and when it was over he nodded once, and then quietly picked up one of my flimsy business cards before indicating he would be in touch.

So excited that I'd had my first 'proper' meeting, I couldn't wait to tell a friend in my group about it. I was horrified when she explained that I'd unknowingly managed to get myself an appointment with the head of one of Eindhoven's mafia groups! In that case ignorance was most definitely bliss; in fact I think it was my saving grace – goodness knows why he agreed to meet me, or what he thought I was going to offer him. To this day I'm curious to know what on earth was going through his mind as I was doing my presentation!

As the months passed I barely saw Mr Ex – he was back in London, figuring out what he wanted to do, spending time with his family and building his business there. In the meantime, I was being taught rude words in Dutch and had had three bikes donated to me. Around this time one of the people in my Dutch network introduced me to a friend of his. We hit it off straight away, and spent many hours sitting on the floor of her apartment – laughing, eating, and getting lost in deep and meaningful conversations around life, astrology, spirituality, and of course, men!

It was amazing; sometimes we would spend hours chatting and then, after I'd cycled home to my place, we'd spend a couple more on the phone! She became my best friend and teacher at the same time – guiding me, pushing me and ALWAYS asking question upon question. I had fallen in love, and her name was Mandena: a truly beautiful woman who would change my life for the better for years to come!

My business was getting there – the network had spread to Belgium and Germany and we had a small team in the UK. I quite liked the hat I was wearing. I had branched off on my own, and was finding my own creative ways to build it up; I had loads of support from the new friends I'd made, and while I was no Donald Trump, I was earning enough to live independently. I was happy and free!

By now I was 20 years old, and with Mr Ex no longer travelling, and calling only when he could sneak a moment away from things, I was certain the relationship had run its course. In the meantime I was slowly becoming very close to a member of my Dutch team, who'd often drop me off at home or join me on long walks. We were both business-obsessed personal-growth addicts, we shared the same taste in music and enjoyed working out. Not the strongest matchmaking list I know, but what can I say? He was moody, mysterious, had blue eyes, and was only seven years my senior!

Anyway, it was only a matter of time before he asked me out on a dinner date. I remember being so excited. He picked the restaurant, opened doors, pulled my chair in and out and translated the menu – he was a true gentleman, my knight in a shiny black sports car! Until, that is, the bill came and he read out my half of it, to the exact cent! I'd heard the phrase 'going Dutch' but I didn't see that coming! At the end of the evening, we exchanged an awkward kiss.

Now you'd imagine I'd have run a mile after this, or that it would at least have set off alarm bells, but no, I was dense – a dry desert of unloved cells, desperate for the next sign of love, even if it was a mirage.

And I was *consciously* dense, too: I could hear my angels shaking their heads, wondering when I was going to get this – as life, God, the Universe, everyone and everything was smacking me over the head – to wake up. Trying to get me to see the lesson sitting right in front of me – the never-ending loop of false love. Something I continuously thought could be found outside of me, in anything on offer – in my case, usually unobtainable and unsuitable men!

And before long I found myself falling in love – again – with someone who was already in a relationship – again – and who probably wouldn't have looked twice at me if it weren't for my small waist, perky breasts and infectious energy and laugh! I thought, *Mary, what is wrong with you?* Mandena was not surprised: despite our conversations I was too blinded by the full rush of chemical emotions that seemed to overtake every part of my body.

But then came the call from Mr Ex. Apparently, *he* had left his wife and he was ready to make a go of our relationship: 'Baby, when are you coming home?!'

~

Remember I said that we can be many things at the same time, in a single moment? Well, that was my relationship with Mr Ex. On the one hand he was a great romantic; he made me feel secure and safe, always cared for and adored. We were both ambitious, too: it wasn't that we wanted to conquer the world and build an empire, more that we liked business; we loved creating something, were both comfortable big-thinkers and in different ways we were doers. We worked – he was the strategy and ideas side; I was the creative who was good with people.

He had old-school values – you make sure your family are safe and well cared for; and I had old-school values – you look after your man, cook for him, keep the home. And I believed that you always had each other's back: even if you disagreed in the outside world you sorted it out behind closed doors. The problem was, I soon found out it doesn't work if you're the only one in the relationship who operates that way.

I was chaotic, he was orderly; I was mature for my age, and he was immature for his. He liked the pub and going out drinking with his friends; I liked to curl up on the sofa with a good book or a movie. He was careful – Mr Safety – I was carefree, oblivious to any potential physical dangers. We were Mr & Ms Entrepreneur, slight risk-takers, big-thinkers, spontaneous and open to the adventure of life.

Neither of us were 'bad' people, but together we were just an utterly disastrous combination that brought out the best and worst in each other – it was almost as if we were two people constantly reflecting their inability to love themselves and therefore unaware of what real love looks like; we were always seeking external guarantees. Our relationship was characterized by a rollercoaster ride of highs and lows, addictions, dramas, break-ups, and passionate make-ups: we were the perfect mess and success, all at the same time!

I felt as if I'd led him on and that I therefore needed to see it through. I never told him I left Holland only because I felt so guilty that he had left his wife for me, and because I was so scared of being on my own in the world. In some ways I did think I loved him, but to be honest, I wouldn't have recognized love if it had hit me in the face and then tattooed itself all over my body.

Ironically, we were at our happiest when we had nothing to our name; nothing save our dreams, our own little bubble of love, ideas, businesses and hopes of the life we would create. My favourite times were when we would lie in bed talking, dreaming, laughing and just cuddling – the real stuff, as I used to call it.

But then, as our bubble grew, so did the cracks, doubts and self-questioning. I felt it was my responsibility to fix it all and try to repair the damage that I, for some reason, took all the blame for. Our individual awareness of self was non-existent.

The first real sign we were in trouble was when I fell pregnant at the age of 22. Turned off by my weight gain, and my inability to show up as the Mary he'd fallen in love with, he had the perfect excuse openly to have an affair with someone we knew – a woman he was hoping to bring in as the next 'nanny' for his kids.

I should have been angrier, or put my foot down more, but I was exhausted. I was drained from running around managing the home, his children – whom I had grown to love as if they were my own – and work. Also, a part of me felt I was being a hypocrite – I felt that somehow it served me right: for hadn't I started off as the 'other woman' too? I wasn't a bad person, so maybe she was the same as me: falling for his charm and smooth tongue. I never really blamed her, or any of the others that came after her.

Also, because I slowly started to notice the all-too-familiar reflection in the other women's eyes – the broken, vulnerable look that said they were desperate for some love and attention; the look that would sadly make you go to any lengths to receive it. I knew that look well, so I felt bad if I punished them; in fact, I preferred to punish myself instead.

Over time my own self-reflection was one of disgust, guilt and immense unhappiness, often relieved by the distraction and drama his affairs with these other women brought – anything to avoid seeing how lost and unhappy I had become. Mr Ex never lied when I asked him whether he'd slept with yet another nanny, friend or passing acquaintance of ours, so I only ever asked when I knew his 'unacceptable' behaviour would bring me the attention I secretly yearned for – knowing his guilt would sometimes mean he'd be extra nice or extra attentive to me. Well, for a short time at least.

It was a controlling, warped and twisted union. At times it would spiral down to terrible lows, resulting in him having several one-night stands, of which a couple led to full-blown affairs. Looking back I don't recognize this Mary who would sit through numerous parties, watching, as he got ridiculously drunk and openly chatted up female guests or hit on friends of ours.

In the early years of our relationship, tired of my weight gain, he'd turn his nose up at me in disgust, or tell me to cover myself up when I wore shorts or a long T-shirt around our home. Sometimes he'd purposely pull back from me when I reached out to him for a hug or some other form of physical comfort. Why? Because he said he thought it would motivate me to lose weight. Looking back, it saddens me that I allowed myself to be treated that way.

Approximately 12 to 18 months after the birth of our son I'd had enough; I hated myself, I hated my life and I hated the thought of doing this for one more day. I was lost, broken and felt so worthless: he had won. Whatever little sense of self I had tried to bring to the table, he'd held it in the palm of his hand and slowly crushed it.

Chapter 6
Bridge Over Troubled Water

*'In spite of everything I shall rise again: I will take
up my pencil, which I have forsaken in my great
discouragement, and I will go on with my drawing.'*
VINCENT VAN GOGH

Have you ever had one of those days when everything suddenly made complete sense? When you felt so calm and so clear that nothing could disturb you? Well, that's exactly how I felt on the day I knew I was going to die.

If someone had been following me around for the previous couple of years, I'm sure they would have said I was suffering from some form of functional depression, post-natal blues, pre-burnout; I don't know which, and at that moment in time I didn't really care. All I knew was that I'd had enough; I was tired – physically, emotionally and mentally – to the core of my bones.

From the outside I appeared to be living a successful and fulfilling life, all by the tender age of 24. Mr Ex and I had just started our own property business, and alongside that, I had started a recruitment agency, which was doing well. I had a beautiful baby boy, who was going to turn two in a few months' time.

I was a part-time mum to three amazing stepsons, all under the age of eight; we had just moved into a lovely town house off a canal, five minutes' walk from London's River Thames, and we were part of a lovely community. So, according to the path of happiness and success, I was well on my way to achieving the 'perfect life'.

The problem was, it didn't feel like it. I'd read so many self-help books by then, attended so many seminars, high-fived more strangers than I'd had hot dinners, and still I wasn't happy. What was wrong with me? I was desperate for the book that told me 'how to stop living the lie', or 'what to do when you supposedly have it all but still feel as if everything is falling apart'.

I hated my body, I was over-worked, my relationship was a farce, I felt I couldn't go to what family I had left for support – and I felt as if I was failing drastically as a mum. I was unhappy, lonely and insecure; and my partner and I were stuck on a never-ending, toxic rollercoaster ride to destruction and back. We'd flip from feeling euphoric to being completely numbed out: both of us oblivious to the disastrous trail we were leaving behind us, as we wore the mask of outward success so well!

So on that early morning, as I crossed Tower Bridge – with the sun shining, the road calm and the light bouncing off the surface of the water – the solution was loud and clear; in fact it felt almost as if I had no choice.

I would like to say this was the first time I'd had such a thought, but it wasn't. Despite my fear of heights I'd had to resist the call of the water on many occasions; today, however, there was no need to rush away from it – to hurry to the other side of the bridge. Today, the heavens knew I was coming. As the sun caressed my cheek, I felt it was a sign – as if the sky was opening, welcoming my imminent arrival.

As I reached the slight recess where the pathway dipped, I looked down at the pushchair: at my beautiful and always happy baby boy. He was going to have to come with me. I couldn't leave him behind – what kind of a mother would that make me? I was the calmest I'd been since his birth as I unstrapped him from his seat, feeling his chubby warm arms surround my neck and his soft brown curls tickle my face. My beautiful baby boy – he was the reason I'd stayed; the reason I was still here…

As I turned towards the side of the bridge, I suddenly thought, *What shall I do with my bag? My wallet? The pushchair?* I hadn't thought about this until that moment: what if someone stole them, emptied my bank account, or worse still, broke into our home? *Mary: you'll be dead in a minute, so why the hell are you worrying about your bag?* But, as bizarre as it sounds, I kept thinking that the last thing I wanted was for my family to hear the news of our passing, and then to find that all our belongings had been stolen, too: that would be too much! *Maybe if I throw the bag in first, I* thought. *It'll sink and then all will be fine.*

No, that would be a waste of money. I looked around to see if I could find a homeless person, or someone who looked as if they could do with some extra cash. *This is stupid*, I thought. *Just take the cards and leave the bag with the other things; whoever needs it, will take it.*

As I started to empty my bag into the bottom of the pushchair the most awful thoughts flooded my body – *What if we don't go at the same time? How can I ensure that he doesn't survive me? What if we get separated on the way down?* Sh%t, Sh%t, Sh%t, I hadn't thought of that.

Maybe I should strap him to my body – gosh, the thought of him surviving with some form of trauma, or brain damage, was too much to bear. Desperately hunting around for his harness, or something to strap him to me, all I could think was that I needed to make sure he was gone before me. Maybe if I pushed his head into my jumper on the way down? That would do it; maybe I should do that now, to make sure? No, better on the way down? Oh God, what am I doing?

As the panic started to rise in my chest, and a light of sanity and reason tried to force its way through my trance, I took a deep breath. *No, this is the right thing. If I'm going to do this I need to do it now.* I knew that too much overthinking would slow me down – and I could feel the increasing presence of a few early risers nearby.

With my baby now tied to me with my belt and a harness strap, and my pockets full of my cards and keys, I made my way to the edge of the wall, once more feeling a sense of calm. As I looked into the dark blue reflective swirls of water, they seemed to promise eternal peace – I knew this was the right and only thing to do.

Okay, but how was I going to get us both onto the side of the bridge without it becoming too obvious? Or my baby falling out of the harness? Up until this point I hadn't considered the limitations of my attire (embarrassed by my size I'd stopped wearing trousers or leggings, and my favoured look was one of perpetual mourning – long black skirts and dresses).

Maybe I needed to move somewhere else; I frantically looked further along the bridge, trying to spot a position that would allow me easier access to the freedom I longed for. Shoot! Now the tourists were out. Frustrated, I wanted to cry out, *Oh, for God's sake!* I never envisioned that this would be so complicated.

I was fat and cumbersome, and the idea of manoeuvring myself with extra baggage was starting to fill me with a mixture of hysteria and panic! I could slowly feel more tourists around me; moving closer – snapping away with their cameras. A handful on the left, two or three on the right. *For God's sake, Mary: why can't you just swallow a handful of pills or drink yourself into a stupor?* Who'd heard of a woman who couldn't throw herself off a bridge because she was too fat! And with that thought, the feeling erupted, but rather than tears, out came the sound of hysterical laughter. It was so loud and full, it made my poor son jump. I just couldn't stop it. Oh my goodness; I was trying not to double over, as the laugh got crazier and crazier, the tears streaming down my face.

Trying to get a grip as more people started to fill the bridge, I took some deep breaths – all the time thinking, *Where the hell are these people coming from?* 'Leave me in peace', I wanted to shout, but the hysterical humour had overtaken me. *Why don't you ask them to give you a hand?* Then the laughter came again, more high-pitched than the last bout.

By this time my son was looking at me as if this were all part of a fun game, giggling and half smiling as he touched my tears. I suddenly felt the shift in my body; the tears were real, my chest started to tighten and I couldn't breathe. Suddenly I could feel the hysteria showing its true colours. I was on the verge of emitting a demonic cackle, whilst trying desperately to breathe and avoid descending into the ultimate, wretched 'ugly cry'. I knew I had to get off the bridge.

—

I quickly grabbed the pushchair and, holding my son awkwardly in one hand and dragging my coat with the other, I hurriedly made my way to the other side, now moving as though my life depended on it. I was horrified and shocked by the thoughts that had so calmly gone through my mind – by the fact that I'd seriously contemplated jumping into the river with my son. What the hell was I thinking?

Turning the corner of the bridge, I stopped at the underpass, strapped my son into his pushchair and gave him his juice. I gently kneeled down, pretending to look for something in the bottom of his seat, and started to sob quietly, and as inwardly as I could – this was a form of crying I'd practised many a time, my whole body shaking, crying out for help. Something had to change, and it had to change *now*.

> *'Your daily life is your school, your temple and your religion.'*
> KAHLIL GIBRAN

My son was now fed, fast asleep and happily none the wiser. As I sat on a little bench on the riverside path, staring out across the water, my eye was drawn to the pretty exteriors of the quaint, high-class restaurants that lined the south side of the Thames. They were all lined up in a neat row, with their expensive signage and inside, their expensive, well-prepared menus to match.

And as I thought about this, I realized that in quality, fine-dining restaurants the chefs spend hours prepping the ingredients for their dishes: carefully sourcing them, making sure they are fresh, and where possible, organic. And this prepping process culminates in the most mouthwatering culinary sensations that leave people wanting more. Restaurant owners and chefs realize that the better the prep, the better the outcome of the dishes.

And that was when I had my first real Wild Awakening moment. I hadn't been doing any prep for my days or my life: I woke up busy, got straight out of bed and hit the ground running; I was constantly on the go until my head hit the pillow at night, exhausted. I was grateful I had so much natural energy, and that I could survive on just four or five hours' sleep a night. But was this really how I wanted to exist? Because that was all it had been to date, just existing – and clearly that was not going very well, given what had just happened on the bridge.

As I sat looking out from what was soon to become my regular riverside spot, I realized I'd settled for the equivalent of a 'fast-food/ takeaway life' with little or no preparation, planning or connection to my days; I'd switch on the machine of functioning, cut open frozen tablets of 'to-dos', chucking every moment into a deep-fat fryer or a microwave, and killing off what little shred of goodness/ life that existed.

That was my life. So I knew if I was going not only to survive this but start to feel happier about my life and myself, I needed to make a commitment – even if it took me the rest of my life to get there, I would strive for a fine-dining life! As I thought about what I might do for my own 'daily prep', I realized that in order for me to really know where I was going wrong, I needed to start paying attention to the little things – making sure I didn't get so far off track that they became the big things, until the big things suffocated me so much that all I wanted to do was drown them out, literally!

And then, on that small bench adjacent to the bridge that had signified my imminent end, I pulled out a pen and paper and started to rewrite my beginning. I needed to raise my awareness; I needed to start using what I had learned, instead of leaving it lying in unread books and wasting away in journals.

So I asked a simple question: Mary: what have you learned about yourself? From your childhood, from your time with Mr Stoner Zen, from the in-depth conversations with Mandena on her living-room floor in Holland; what have you learned from this current relationship; all the books, the workshops and the people you have met along the way? What have you learned about yourself?

And there began the long journey towards what would eventually become my 'Daily Prep' – the 9 Questions and an accompanying set of actions that have genuinely ended up saving my life!

~

I would like to say that on the morning after the 'bridge' incident I started working on myself furiously every day, until I finally found my self-worth and self-love tucked in my back pocket, pulled them out like a superhero's cape and flew off to become a stronger, more positive woman!

Yeah, right! This was the real world...

In reality it took several more years and a lot more highs and lows – including an almost year-long separation – before Mr Ex and I began to find steady ground and get to a point in the relationship where we both saw and accepted each other for who we were. So when I say that finding yourself and really working on yourself is not an overnight process, I mean it. To find some sort of normality and a sense of self took time, and I had to do the work on my own. I had even lost touch with Mandena – there's a lesson in that I'm sure – I can feel her smiling as I write.

Towards the end of my relationship with Mr Ex we had an honest conversation about the affairs, the women and his feelings for me.

He spoke of how, before we got together, he'd watch me through his office window as I arrived for work – a 19-year-old girl, chaotically bouncing across the courtyard in front of the building; I was usually late, still dressed in my gym gear from my early morning workout. I was full of smiles and laughter, happy and chatty to everyone as I entered. Full of life, he said.

Despite the affairs I knew he adored me – he was always showing me, in his way, how much he loved me and his little family. I saw that he worked hard to provide for us, and I saw that, towards the end, he was very remorseful about his behaviour earlier in the relationship. But given that he'd always insisted he couldn't imagine a life without me, I could never quite work out why he'd failed to stop it, and nor could he; in fact, he likened it to some form of addiction.

Sadly, by the time we reached the place we were so desperate to get to, I realized I was no longer in love with him and was no longer growing or learning in that space. We loved each other as people: for what we had been through and what we potentially thought we could be. But I woke up one day and realized our entire, 18-year relationship had been a very long wait for that potential to be realized. We'd become co-parenting mates who worked well together. Perfect, but empty!

In July 2010, knowing it was unfair on him and unfair on myself to continue to live a lie, I sat down and told him it was time to call it a day. I knew I needed to start growing up and standing on my own two feet. I also knew that we both deserved to be with someone who would love us for who we are – not who they hoped we would eventually become.

It was a very painful end, but a liberating and scary start to the next chapter of my life. But with seven of my 9 Questions already in place, a hell of a lot of trust, some great friends to support me and a reconnection with Mandena through a bizarre series of events, I was ready to grow up, leaving behind one of my most powerful and greatest teachers on love. A man who to this day I still love dearly!

Part 11

My Wild Awakening: Finding the 9 Questions

Introduction

*'Our soul's desire to know itself is ultimately what
drives our internal compass – it's our hard-wiring,
our in-built GPS system. It's always re-routing us and
directing us back to our original end destination:
back to the lessons we need to learn, and ultimately,
back to the journey of discovering our "self".'*

Welcome to Part II – where I tell you all about the wild, intense and crazy journey I took on the way to discovering the 9 Questions. As I explained in Part I, after the incident on the bridge, I realized that I needed to come up with a practice I could do every morning that would 'prep' me for the day ahead – something that would put me in the right frame of mind so I could enjoy as many moments of it as possible.

In my search for what this practice could look like, I started to ask myself some serious questions – about my life, who I was, and what I really wanted. Questions I knew I needed to start answering, if I wasn't to keep making the same mistakes over and over again, and potentially end up back on that bridge. So, I thought about what I needed to ask myself, and as I slowly uncovered those 9 key Questions, it was as if each one opened a doorway to a whole new way of looking at myself, of being, of connecting to my life – almost like themes, or a soundtrack to my life.

As asking the 9 Questions began to become part of my daily routine, I realized I needed to add some other actions around them, things that would help me to really connect with my answers. Over time, it became apparent that I needed to slow down more often; meditate more; spend time connecting with nature; exercise as often as possible, and throughout Part II I explain how I came to learn that these things were important for me. Today, all of these actions, plus answering the 9 Questions, have become what I call my Daily Prep (there's more about this in Part III).

The 9 Questions have gone on to provide me with some profound awakenings and lessons in all areas of my life – from my love life to my relationships with my family and friends; from my work to my role as a parent; and from my body image to my mental and emotional wellbeing – and I have shared many of these with you in the following pages. And while I won't be telling you what to do with your own life in this section, for you to get anything worthwhile from this book, it's vital that you read Part II before embarking on your own Wild Awakening journey. There are no quick fixes to changing our lives, or shortcuts on the road to finding ourselves.

Finally, I must stress that everything I've shared with you in this section is based on my own personal experiences and my *present* level of awareness, which is continuously deepening, expanding and growing. So please go with what resonates with you and challenge, skip or stay open to anything that doesn't; there is no right or wrong here, and I don't own the copyright to 'truth'.

All I ask is that you remain open-minded until the end, and allow yourself to be surprised. Because you never know what might spark a powerful Wild Awakening – an 'aha' moment – that could change the direction of your life forever. Have fun!

Chapter 1

Higher Ground

'Other animals make their livings by living,
but people work like crazy, thinking that
they have to in order to stay alive.'
MASANOBU FUKUOKA – THE ONE-STRAW REVOLUTION

'Have you heard of Fukuoka?' the man was asking me.

Fuku who? I thought. I was exhausted, and I couldn't register what he was saying. I'd just arrived at Tribewanted Monestevole – a small sustainable community living on a beautiful fifteenth-century farm in Umbria, Italy – following an invitation from a friend to see whether my organization could run retreats there.

But, in the lead-up to the trip, I'd gone two days without sleep (this had become the story of my life), and in my bag were piles of paperwork. During the flight, I'd been so out of it, I'd even managed to enter a deep sleep while sitting on the loo! All quite ironic, really – the co-director of a mind-body-spirit organization about to hit burnout. And not very Zen!

My friend, who had recently become part of the team at Tribewanted, hurried over and interrupted our conversation: 'This is Mary,' she said to the man. 'She's one of the directors at Alternatives.' I loved it that she seemed so excited to introduce me to this guy, but I didn't really get why an Italian 'perma-something' gardener would be interested in my organization. And although I knew she was coming from a great space, I was done in.

S*&t, you're tall! I thought, looking up at his long frame. I suddenly realized that most of these words had actually slipped out of my mouth, but luckily the swearing got lost in the handshakes! I smiled weakly, but all I could hear was my internal voice saying, *Mary, you need to get to your room. SLEEP!*

'I'm running a workshop on permaculture later, if you're interested?' Mr Italy continued. (Clearly his name wasn't Mr Italy, but you've seen the way my unimaginative identity-hiding goes by now!) *Oh God, isn't that gardening?* I thought. He was cute, but not *that* cute. By then I'd reached the stage where my body was saying to me: *If you don't sleep now, Mary, I'm just going to collapse on the floor.*

'Sure…what time?' I found myself saying. Of course I did. (According to Dan Millman's book about numerology, *The Life You Were Born to Live*, I'm a 29/11, and basically, these are people-pleasers, over-givers; we are the ones who can't say 'no' when someone asks us to do something. What else? Ah yes – we have issues with boundaries, we over-cooperate, and then, when we feel as if we've been taken for granted, we completely withdraw!)

So I stood there like the little coward I was: hearing myself agree to go, but secretly knowing that as soon as I hit my room I was going straight to bed. An hour later, as I struggled to keep myself upright on the chair, I was filled with disbelief: how on earth had I allowed my friend to change my mind, and talk me into attending this gardening workshop? *Mary, you really need to sort your life out!*

'Mary, he will be really upset if you don't go!' she'd pleaded. Hmm, I wasn't convinced he'd even notice, but I thought, *Mary: do it for her.* After all, this was a new job for her, and I was so proud she'd managed to attract such a wonderful opportunity in Italy. Plus, the timing of the trip had been great for me on a personal level: I'd needed to get out of the office and London, to escape the mounting pressures of my job.

So, despite my exhaustion, I'd agreed to attend the talk on the practices and principles of permaculture. As I sat there, trying not to think about the gorgeous handmade bed awaiting me in my room, I resigned myself to enduring what I figured would be the longest hour of my life. I decided I needed something that would hold my attention. And *voilà*, there he was, leading the class – Mr Italy himself.

As he drew a weird-looking tree on the board, I settled my gaze. *This will do nicely*, I thought. *Perhaps this workshop won't be so bad after all!* As I was debating whether to tune in to Mr Italy's rich, slightly mixed Italian accent or slowly work my eyes up and down his physique, my attention suddenly seemed to have other ideas, as it started to engage with what he was saying.

As diagrams of trees and images of earthworms and soil appeared, bizarrely, I became more and more hooked. Then he started to talk about things like 'care for the Earth, care for the planet, and don't use more than you need'. And although I was desperate to return to studying his body, I simply couldn't – it seemed that the focus of my free entertainment had changed. Every cell in me was awakening to this thing called permaculture.

This was clearly more than just food and farming. Mr Italy was talking about something called 'humus' (it turned out he wasn't referring to the Middle Eastern dish made out of chickpeas!) and clay, and the entire ecosystem of living organisms working away right underneath our feet. I couldn't understand why I was starting to feel so energized – it was as if my body was coming home, unlocking information buried deep in my cells. It was as if I had known about all this for years.

Sensing my sudden engagement, Mr Italy started to turn his attention towards me: as if a knowing part of us knew that an important message needed to be delivered. As my excitement grew, my mind began to imagine a world in which everyone lived this way – mirroring the same simple, natural cycles of Mother Nature. All of us living together: accepting our differences and personal needs, but in complete harmony with our environment.

Working together as part of a well-oiled 'community' – taking only what we needed and only having to *do* what was necessary. There would be no work pressure, stress, bills to pay; we'd be living off the land, enjoying the space. We'd be well fed, and entertained by rich conversation and just the joy of being alive and hanging out with like-minded people. We'd be free of the controlling ties of a system designed merely to support a system. How come I'd never heard of this 'permaculture' thing?!

'So, any more questions?' Mr Italy asked at the end of the talk. I put up my hand and the questions started to flow. After 20 minutes of back and forth, both of us completely forgetting anyone else was in the room, I finally asked: 'So, when can we visit the gardens?' My physical exhaustion was long forgotten!

The next morning after breakfast, not wanting to miss a single moment of finding out more, I trotted down to the gardens. I was the first to arrive, so I had a wander around, trying to soak up everything we'd been taught the day before. Ten minutes later I heard a tuk-tuk sound and what I can only describe as a three-wheeled mini motorcycle truck came down the path. Its driver, Mr Italy, squeezed out of the small compartment – smiling, happy and slightly surprised to see a student there so early.

'Is there anything I can do to help?' I asked – not sure how far the 'get stuck in and become a part of our community' policy extended. 'Sure, you wanna to do something right now?' he replied.

I nodded, so he held out a crate containing some gardening tools and said, 'Grab this and come with me.' As we walked over to a long planting bed containing green beans, I took a deep breath in and absorbed the stunning views of the mountains that surrounded the gardens. Mr Italy knelt down next to the first row of beans and showed me the point on the stalk where each bean should be picked; he then explained which beans should be left and which should be given back to the earth.

Half an hour later, as we worked our way down the rows, the conversation was flowing. We shared what had come up in yesterday's talk; what it was like to work for a spiritual organization; what true spirituality and consciousness meant, and how he'd got into permaculture. As we swung from meaningful conversation to deep bursts of silliness and jokes, I was transfixed. Before I left, I thanked Mr Italy for what had been a magical morning and promised I would be back the next day.

When I awoke the following morning I felt so alive – it was as if the weight of the city was happily being absorbed by the land: replacing my cells with pure life force. I was tingling from head to toe. From its warm, friendly 'at home' environment to its stunning views of nature at its finest, this place had me hooked.

As I sat on the kitchen step putting on my shoes, Filippo, the owner, popped his head out the door: 'You okay?' he asked. 'Oh, yes,' I breathed. 'This place is amazing.' Proud to receive such positive feedback, and, I think, keen that I get a sense of the real concept behind the place, Filippo stayed to chat.

It was fascinating to hear first-hand what they were trying to achieve at Tribewanted, and to learn of their hopes of becoming an example of what truly sustainable living could look like in 50 years' time: not just in remote locations, but also in developing countries. I loved their wider vision to create ecotourism, and their desire to expand and become a part of communities around the world.

Floating, and ready to sell everything I owned to be able to live here – or even just stay here for another week – I turned towards the gardens. I was happy: hop, skip and jumping to my favourite part of the grounds, delighting in the knowledge that there was more than enough work to fill my trip!

When I arrived, Mr Italy was watering the plants. Smiling, he threw me a spray containing a white silky liquid, which I later discovered was his homemade soap. We headed over to the rows of courgettes, green beans and lettuce, all intermingled and growing around each other.

'So you just plant everything together?' I asked. 'Yes, that's the beauty of permaculture – it's about allowing everything to coexist in a natural way, each balancing the other out. It's a harmonious community of fruit and veg.' *I love this*, I thought: all coexisting together naturally. Unlike us humans, sadly.

I pulled on some gloves and got to work. Now usually I wouldn't have been seen dead doing this: I had a garden back home, but I hadn't set foot in it for 18 months! So this trip was a revelation in so many ways. As I slowly worked my way down the row, I started to find the gloves quite cumbersome. So, reckoning I could just about hold the tips of the beans, I discarded the gloves – the thick barrier between my fingers and life.

I happily settled down to this rather meditative task. For some reason I found it comforting to spray and massage the stems of the plants and, unusually, I was completely unfazed by all the little beetle-like aphids that were crawling on them.

What's happening to me? I thought. Something felt different inside; it was a feeling I hadn't felt before. As I continued I suddenly started to notice the spiders – long ones, thin ones, tiny ones. The city Mary, with her spider phobia, would have been jumping up and down and screaming by now, but this Mary, the 'possessed by Mother Nature' one, seemed completely undisturbed, almost fascinated. She watched as one tiny creature seemed to look up at her, almost studying her – as fascinated by this big face and wide eyes as she was with its miniature features.

Then, out of the blue, the freakiest thing happened: suddenly I was looking up at myself – seeing myself, almost feeling myself – but with the sense that I was the spider and the spider was me. *We were no different from each other.* Then, as a spider climbed onto a bean, I looked at the bean and I *felt* it: the life of the bean and the life of me. I just felt life – vibrating, pulsating through my body. I felt alive and I felt life, and I mean *really* felt the life of everything. I felt it in my cells, in my blood, in my core; I felt everything; I was everything: I was the spider and the spider was me.

Mr Italy suddenly smiled and called over: 'Everything okay?' I looked up at him, unable to describe what I was feeling and experiencing. I managed a 'Yes, I feel great.' Almost laughing now at this misplaced city girl, Mr Italy knelt opposite me and we slowly carried on with the gardening. He somehow knew that the Mary in the garden was – and wasn't – a very different one to the Mary who had happily been gassing away the day before.

A few days later, as I said my farewells to Monestevole, I reflected on my short, but timeless and transformative, stay. I realized I had not only fallen in love with life again, I had fallen in love with a part of myself I never knew existed. It was almost as if I was waking up to this part of myself, my awareness expanding.

Back in London, I felt deeply depressed: I struggled with the noise, the pollution, the pace of life, and the mounting number of emails and rising stress levels. I missed the clean air, the stunning mountain views, the mad community. It had been a surreal trip: what with the farm animals, the unnecessary and necessary dramas, the constant smells of Italian food.

Returning to my desk at Alternatives, in what I affectionately call our little broom cupboard of an office in the heart of London, was incredibly hard, especially after I'd had so many insightful, funny, spiritual and often philosophical chats in Monestevole around what it really means to live consciously. So I decided to integrate as much as I could of what I'd learned and experienced there into my own life.

And, looking for any excuse to continue my conversations with Mr Italy, I decided to inbox-stalk him. A few email chats later, I was sat with a simple reading list and a modest plan of action. Mr Italy suggested that I take my time and introduce things slowly. Little did he know that I never do things slowly, take my time, or do as I am told. I was a woman with a new mission – to find out as much as I could about permaculture!

Two months later, I attended a mini permaculture course in Stepney City Farm in the heart of London. Our teacher, Kevin Mascarenhas, was great – I'd never met anyone who was so excited to share his knowledge. In fact, he is one of the few people I've met who has mirrored my internal excitement *externally*. I'd just finished reading *The One-Straw Revolution* by Masanobu Fukuoka, and was on fire – that book had connected with me in so many ways, and had brought the wider concepts of permaculture – its amazing holistic principles – full circle.

Permaculture isn't just about food growth or agriculture: it's a whole way of being. It's about living in alignment with ourselves, others and Mother Nature – our natural teacher. For me, this was about a whole new shift in consciousness – something I'd been opening up to in the months following my trip to Italy. And being around passionate people – from the team at Tribewanted to Kevin – excited me; I couldn't get enough of them. I was buzzing.

That evening, after the class, I looked through the small handful of baby photos one of my brothers had so kindly dug out and copied for me as a Christmas present. Among them was a shot of the garden at my foster parents' house. I remembered then how my foster dad had always given me seeds to plant. And then I knew why. There it was: Daddy was naturally doing permaculture, and I'd been helping him!

QUESTION 1:
What have I learned about myself?

> 'Every mammal on this planet… develops a natural
> equilibrium with the surrounding environment, but you
> humans do not. You move to an area, and you multiply…
> until every natural resource is consumed. There is another
> organism that follows the same pattern: a virus.'
>
> AGENT SMITH – THE MATRIX

The first of the 9 Questions is all about self-awareness: knowing ourselves at the deepest level. It's about asking ourselves who we are without the labels or the masks, or the games we play to make people like us or to control a situation. What is it that makes us do the things we do, behave the way we behave, or make the decisions and choices that constantly shape our lives? What are the streams of thought that are affecting our emotions – making us happy, or potentially bringing us pain and suffering?

When I sat down at the side of that bridge, having reached my all-time low, I instinctively knew that if things were going to change, I needed to start paying closer attention to how I was living my life on a day-to-day basis. And while I've been asking myself Question 1 since the bridge incident, my trip to Italy made me realize that I hadn't actually been *observing* myself as I did so – but rather *judging* myself.

I'd been taking the things I'd learned about myself and grouping them into 'good' and 'bad'. For example, I'd say: *I've learned that I'm very good at motivating a team*, and *I've learned that I'm really bad at doing x, y, z*. I'd been answering the Question with a very critical eye instead of an observational one, listing all my faults and the things I needed to improve.

That moment in Italy – when I saw that I was the spider and the spider was me, we were just observing each other – I realized there was no good or bad, there was just the moment and 'what is'. So that's when I knew I needed to alter my approach to Question 1: I've learned that in order for us to really know anything about ourselves, we have to *observe not judge* who we are and how we're behaving.

So, without passing judgment or making assumptions, I kept asking, *What have I learned about myself? Who is this person I see in the mirror before me?* And as the answers started to flow, I pulled out my journal and began to write things like this: *I've learned that I am most alive when I feel free to do my own thing. I've learned that when I agree to do things I don't really want to do, it becomes very messy.*

Below I've shared some of the powerful lessons and insights I've discovered or experienced on a deeper level since I started asking myself Question 1. As you read through them, if you have any Wild Awakenings – or 'aha' moments – of your own, make a note of them, and when you start to work through the 9 Questions yourself, which I'll show you how to do in Part III, you can explore what came up for you.

And remember that what follows is based simply on my personal experiences and on my *present* level of awareness, which is continuously deepening, expanding and growing. So please go with what works for you, and if you decide you want to challenge, skip, or stay open to anything that doesn't, then feel free: it's your choice.

I need to stop, face the music and feel again

I've learned that, in the past, every time I faced a challenge, I'd just keep on swimming through it, no matter painful it was to do that.

A few years ago, I started to realize I was a bit like the little fish Dory in the movie *Finding Nemo*: every time I faced a challenging situation or event, I'd just keep swimming through it. Maybe it'd knock me out for a moment, or a few hours, or sometimes a day, but then I'd get straight back up and just keep swimming.

In some respects this way of being kept me alive, but in other ways I can see that it also numbed me out. For example, at one point, I'd spend all of my free time watching movies (sometimes three or four, back to back). I'd also overeat and over-exercise (when I was a teenager I'd work out demonically in the gym – two hours in the morning before school and then another two hours after school). While I was still at school, I became addicted to painkillers – sometimes taking so many I'd throw up.

I'd never given myself the space or time to process fully what had happened to me as a child, and I could see that I was continuously repeating the same mistakes, over and over again. I was becoming more reactive than proactive. There were moments when I knew I needed to slow down and start paying closer attention to my life, but for some reason I just couldn't seem to find the time.

So when I finally *did* start to slow down (or should I say when life itself slowed me down) and I got to *really* observe myself – as if I were a scientific experiment or something in nature that had caught my eye – I was quite saddened by what I saw.

I started to notice things about myself, about certain aspects of my personality. I saw the way that my insecurity, low self-esteem and lack of self-love were playing out in my life. I tried very hard to remain in a place where I wouldn't continuously judge myself, or come to conclusions about myself based on preconceived ideas or conditioned assumptions, but I won't lie, it was very hard. I knew it was time to face the music and allow the healing process to begin.

I need to slow down and reconnect with myself

I've learned that the more I slow down, the easier my life becomes, and the easier it is to hear the lessons I need to 'get', or see about myself, in order to grow.

I've learned that life is our greatest teacher and that the things I most need to learn about myself are playing out right in front of me, all the time. My life lessons, as I like to call them, can be very subtle, and because I used to rush around in a very disconnected state, not always paying close enough attention to things, I'd very often miss them.

I've noticed that the more I fail to see what's right in front of me – what I most need to learn – the louder the signals get for me to slow down. Eventually, the message I need to wake up to starts to feel like a bruise that's being punched, over and over again. This completely knocks me out, either physically (through illness or exhaustion) or emotionally; or it totally overwhelms me until I can't think properly or clearly see what's next.

But part of me resists slowing down – mainly because there are aspects of myself I've struggled to accept; I've not always liked what I've seen, and I've often judged myself harshly. On the occasions I did manage to slow down, I'd start to see how unhappy I was with certain areas of my life, and if you work on the basis that everything that's happening in our lives is a reflection of what's going on inside us, then that unhappiness was ultimately within me.

I can see that I was afraid of being on my own; afraid of being still, quiet. My goodness, the idea of sitting still for even half an hour, just with my inner thoughts and feelings, used to terrify me. However, in the wake of my trip to Italy last year, I've started to spend more time in nature, and to meditate more often, and I'm now enjoying the immediate benefits of slowing down.

I've started to feel much more comfortable in my own skin, and I'm no longer afraid of spending time on my own; in fact, at times I can even say I enjoy it. (Note: spending time alone is not the same as resting or having some downtime; it's when you are completely alone – when you aren't using a mobile device, talking to anyone or doing things virtually.)

I'm also noticing that my understanding of myself, and my ability to 'get' things, is speeding up – it's almost as if my awareness is taking on a life of its own. So it's now more noticeable when I'm unplugged and disconnected than when I feel connected. The more I slow down, the easier life becomes – it's as if by creating more space between my thoughts and my actions, I'm finding it easier to work out what I really want, and feel more connected to my decisions. It's not that I don't get upset, or feel pain and hurt, but the more I understand the source of these feelings, the easier it is to deal with them.

Now I'm not suggesting that I'm floating around in a state of continuous bliss – trust me, if that were the case my life would be very different. I still experience ups and downs, just as we all do – sometimes I feel as if I'm all over the place, and other times I'm really engaged. But what I've learned is, instead of numbing out what's happening, I need to try to *understand* what's going on. I need to allow the pain of what I'm feeling to rise to the surface – and that's something I never would have done in the past.

We don't need to overcomplicate things!

I've learned that life is simple: it is we who make it complicated.

Recently, Alternatives hosted a workshop by mind-body-spirit educator William Bloom, called 'How to Teach and Lead Meditation'. At one point, an attendee asked: 'What does it mean if you fall asleep during your mediation?' To which William replied, 'Well, there are two reasons for this: your body may be processing something quite painful that's perhaps too much for you, or quite traumatic.'

'And the second reason?' the man asked.

'You are tired,' William replied.

I burst out laughing at this. *Genius*, I thought. (I do love William).

One of the things that's really becoming apparent to me is that life is not that complicated, and the rules are pretty simple. It's true that our conditioning can make it hard for us to understand what's driving some of our behaviour – sometimes we'll do one thing when we really want to do something else. However, if we raise our awareness (by bringing our attention into the moment as much as possible) and are open to some honest self-enquiry, it's not that hard to start seeing the patterns and the roots of most of our decision-making processes.

I just need to ask for what I want

I've learned that I need to ask for what I want,
and keep it simple, keep it clear.

After my trip to Tribewanted, Mr Italy and I eventually became Skype buddies. We'd talk for hours about each other's lives, the things that were inspiring us, moving us – sustainability, corruption in society, permaculture, spirituality, relationships: basically, anything and everything.

We'd catch up with each other after work practically every other day, and if we weren't speaking we'd be texting, emailing or touching base in some other way. It's crazy how we found the time to talk so much, but we'd both become full-on self-growth junkies – each of us fast learners and completely open to the process.

In fact, for about four or five months we were like two kids in a self-discovery candy shop – stuffing ourselves with knowledge, over-analysing every twitch and emotion in our bodies, exploring the deeper meaning of things until we metaphorically threw up. But then, after a period of quite intense dialoguing, I suddenly didn't hear from him for a while. To me, this felt really strange, and totally out of sync with how we'd been before.

A few more days of silence passed, and I started to think, *I wonder if he's okay? Maybe he got bored? Did I piss him off? Should I call him? No, I'd better not: he's probably busy... I might disturb him. He probably needs some space.* A real, full-on, runaway mind filled with insecure thoughts.

Eventually, rather than just calling him and asking if he was around for a chat – something I would have told a friend to do in a similar situation – I took the coward's way out and emailed him. It was a gentle, subtle nudge; the addict trying to avoid revealing she was suffering from withdrawal symptoms. Still no response. *Hmm, this is very unlike him*, I thought.

I left it for a bit longer, and then thought, darn it, I'll send him an SMS. But this is me, remember: I didn't just send him a normal, simple message. No, mine was a ridiculous, long-winded, round the houses SMS; but still there was no response. Now at this point I was starting to get annoyed: the kind of 'how dare he?' annoyed. Then the following day, Mr Italy replied: he was tired, he said.

Well, I was not happy – why hadn't he just said so, instead of ignoring me? I sent him a message that heavily hinted at this, and after a few heated exchanges back and forth, he suddenly said, 'Why didn't you just message me and say you wanted to chat?' And bingo, there it was – the million-dollar simple bloody question! Why didn't I just say, 'Are you free to talk?' No story, no fuss – just as a child would do. Remember when we were kids and life was simple? We'd communicate using direct questions like:

'Do you want to be my friend?'

'Can I play with you?'

'Do you want to come round to my house for tea?'

'Do you like me?'

Really, how simple is that? And when we see it, we love it! It makes us laugh and warms our hearts, because our souls yearn for that simplicity again. We all just want a simple life, and I believe that on some level we actually crave it. But as 'grown-ups' so many of us turn the simplest thing into something so complicated. It's as if we're afraid to be honest, to be 'vulnerable' – as if that's some form of weakness.

Anyway, Mr Italy and I had a good laugh about this incident later. He admitted that he'd wanted to teach me a lesson for not simply asking for what I wanted, and instead, second-guessing what was going on. In fact, I could quietly hear his unspoken words: *Mary, you are such a disaster!* This was an expression he'd started using. Initially, I didn't get it, and it actually annoyed me, but now it makes me laugh, because I've come to understand that it's his way of saying that sometimes I come at things in such a crazy way, it's almost as if I'm an emotional mess (what could possibly have given him that idea!?)

I need to tame my monkey mind

I've learned that in order to experience true peace
in my life, I need to manage my monkey mind.

Are you familiar with the Buddhist term 'monkey mind'? It's a metaphor that's used to describe the incessant chatter and commentary that goes on in our heads: the never-ending questioning, second-guessing, worrying, churning, mental decision-making; the to-do lists, the thoughts about what that person said about us... and what we want to say to the person who upset us... and the 'how dare he not call me back?' On and on it goes, constantly.

Well, I came to realize that I had a full-on group of monkeys chattering away in my mind. What's the collective noun for a group of monkeys? Come on, Mary (sneakily Googling it: 'troop, barrel, cartload, tribe'). That's what I had – a tribe of monkeys, running wild! And I knew that if I wanted to find *any* peace in my life, I needed to rein them in and sort out my internal chaos, as some of my thoughts were making me so anxious, I literally couldn't focus on a thing!

After a while I found that meditation, connecting to and being in nature, listening to chillout or meditative music – even the sounds of nature – have really helped calm my mind. And in the end a part of me accepts that on some level I'll probably never entirely get rid of my crazy thoughts – we all have them, but what I can do is choose which ones I focus on and give my attention to, and which ones I let run by.

For if truth be told, no thought really 'belongs to us' or is unique to us: they all come from the universal soup of thoughts! We just borrow them, sometimes recycle them, and every now and then we become overly obsessed with them. (It's a bit like that film where the woman ties the man to the bed. *Misery*: that's the one. Great film! Anyway, that's how we can be with some of our crazy thoughts: like the woman in *Misery*, hanging onto them and never letting them go. Ah well, we are only human.)

Meditation, exercise and being in nature are important to me

I've learned that meditation is not just about sitting in a fixed position and breathing deeply – there are many ways to reach a meditative state. Meditation is about the way we choose to live our lives.

Determined to manage my constant mind chatter, slow down, reconnect and bring more 'me' into my day, I decided to put together a few practices that I could do before asking myself the 9 Questions. These became: meditation, exercise, and being in nature. During my research into meditation techniques, I came across these words by the US spiritual teacher Adyashanti: 'One of the keys to being really free is to live in the same way as you meditate. When we really allow everything to be as it is, that's a very fertile space – a very potent state of consciousness.'

Funnily enough, it didn't sound as if he was referring to the meditation technique I was practising at the time, which consisted of sitting half-upright on my bed, eyes closed, trying hard not to fall asleep or constantly think about hot sex; in fact, if I were to live my life in the same way as I meditate, I would be horizontal for most of the time! I guess inner calm is inner calm, though, however you get there ;-)

Anyway, with the help of Adyashanti's book *True Meditation*, and Dan Millman's *The Life You Were Born to Live*, I really started to notice and join the dots between my blocked energy (which came when I was feeling stuck or frustrated: usually because I was doing things I didn't want to do), my creativity (something I experience an abundance of when I'm aligned and really on track with what feels good for me), and my weight gain (something I was learning was a form of protection).

The more I read, the more I started to raise my awareness of the times I was out of my flow – disconnected from myself. I really started to notice how dramatic those shifts would be when I stopped doing my Daily Prep, and I was also starting to notice that whatever I was experiencing on the inside (turmoil, chaos, separation from the real me), I would also experience on the outside, in my day-to-day life. This is something that is called mirroring – when your external world reflects, or mirrors, your internal world.

I've learned that when things are a mess on the outside, it means that things are normally messy on the inside too – in terms of my thoughts, my emotions, and my body. I've seen that meditation, exercise and being in nature are great ways to calm me down, as they allow me to reconnect and create a more meditative state as I go about my day.

I hide behind busyness

I've learned that being 'too busy' can be a cleverly constructed, socially acceptable cover-up we use to avoid the things we don't want to see, or are not ready to deal with.

This has been quite a poignant lesson for me, as it took me a while to realize that being 'too busy' was another way I'd avoid dealing with my emotions, or the feelings that I just didn't want to see or was finding too overwhelming.

I accept there can be genuine busyness, and there are times in my life when I am that, but I've noticed a pattern of becoming almost continuously 'too busy', and that has followed me through most of my life. At times I've worn it proudly, like a little badge (a bit like the Baby on Board badges London Underground hand out to pregnant women using the Tube, only mine says: 'Sorry, too busy!')

This tendency goes back a long way: I remember my best friend from school ever so gently saying once: 'Mary, have you ever wondered whether this rushing around all the time is you hiding from things you might not want to look at?' At the time I knew she was right, but ironically I had neither the time nor the energy to look at it. Until I started to notice that people would apologize before they asked me for anything: 'Sorry to disturb you, Mary...' or 'I know you are really busy, but...'

Being busy was my infallible shield, my protection and my excuse not to be still. I woke up busy, hit the day busy and crashed every evening busy. Sometimes my then partner and I (Mr Ex) would even have busy sex – going through the motions but not always really present to each other's needs; just going for the release.

The problem was, I was busying my way to burnout, and when I finally gave myself some time and stripped back the layers I could see that being busy meant I could avoid feeling the pain of everything I'd experienced; that being busy meant I didn't have to look at the scars left by my messed-up childhood, relationships and sense of self.

So as soon as I became more aware of this – which was not that long ago – I started to schedule myself back into my diary. I'd make time for myself, slow down and also do one simple thing I loved, even if it was just reading a chapter from my favourite book. As Julia Cameron says in her book *The Artist's Way*, I'd date myself. And that, along with my Daily Prep (the 9 Questions, meditation, exercise, being still, and connecting with nature), seems slowly to be doing the trick!

WILD AWAKENING WISDOM

- I've learned that the more I slow down, the easier it is for me to see and understand why I'm making certain decisions.

- I've learned that life isn't that complicated: we just make it so.

- I've learned that being 'too busy' all the time can be a way of avoiding the things we either don't want to see or are not really ready to deal with.

- I've learned that in order to experience true peace in my life, I need to look at how much attention I give to my thoughts, and not let my thoughts and emotions rule me!

- I've learned that meditation is not just about sitting cross-legged and breathing deeply. It's about how we choose to connect to every moment of every day; basically, how we live our lives.

Chapter 2

True Colours

*'The first step toward change is awareness.
The second step is acceptance.'*

<small>NATHANIEL BRANDEN</small>

I love my mum and I'm very, very proud of her, but it wasn't always that way. The other day I called her to wish her a happy birthday, and to tell her how sorry I was that I couldn't be there in person. (I must admit that I'm not as good at giving birthday cards and gifts as I used to be.) My mum shared that she'd had a lovely day. She'd just finished watching the movie adaptation of the classic novel *Jane Eyre*. She asked me if I'd read the book; I told her I had, and that I really enjoy watching period dramas and films.

Mum then confessed that she'd found *Jane Eyre* very beautiful and romantic, and that it was now one of her favourite films. I laughed affectionately at this. But then she said, quite abruptly, in the all-too-familiar, 'get away with you' voice I fondly remember from my childhood: 'What? Do you think I don't like those kinds of films, too?' I laughed again, and said: 'Mum – sometimes it hits me how little I know you.'

'What makes you think I'm any different to you?' she retorted, half joking, half frustrated at the way 'we children' continue to see her as just our 'mum' – overlooking the other sides of her: the whole woman with her own hopes, dreams, enjoyment and desires. All those things that she'd carried before and after she'd had us.

As my mother spoke, I became aware of the false judgments I still carried and sometimes placed on her. Although we've been on a great journey of acceptance and 'getting to know each other' in recent years, I'll sometimes default to the version of her I feared as a child, as opposed to the one who stands before me today.

When I was growing up I always compared the way Mum and I were with each other with the relationships my friends had with their mums. At times I was shocked at the way some of my friends behaved towards their mothers: they'd speak to them in such an insolent way, slam doors in their faces, make ridiculous demands and use the kind of language that in our house would risk certain death! But despite all that, my friends enjoyed something special with their mothers that I didn't.

I felt this most acutely when I spent time at my best friend's house. I envied the tenderness I saw between her and her mum, and the way they would sometimes go shopping together, or touch base around each other's day. And while I really valued so many aspects of my own upbringing – the independence it gave me, and the strength; the ability to stand on my own two feet; the respect and manners I learned to show towards others; the way we were taught not to take anything for granted – I wanted that tenderness too.

I recently spoke to my mum about this and she explained that things had been so different in her youth; she herself hadn't experienced the things I was talking about. She loved her mum, she said, but didn't grow up knowing her mum loved her; however there was no need to speak of it. But as a child, what I felt was missing seemed normal to me: it was something I saw my friends receiving unconditionally and I wanted it too.

I longed to have that kind of mother-daughter relationship – one that provided a safe, go-to place – as I navigated the challenging transition from adolescence to womanhood. All those physical changes, and the rollercoaster emotions; and at times just needing to know I was loved and okay. I remember how long it took me to figure out that I needed my first bra; I borrowed one from my older sister at one point, clueless about the importance of getting a proper fitting.

I think I just desperately needed some help as I went through those physical, emotional and social rites of passage: I guess in the same way that all young girls do (especially in today's fast-changing world). Figuring these things out on your own can be scary.

When things came out about my father's abuse, my relationship with my mother took a different turn. I'd confided in one of my teachers at school, who intervened and brought in social services. I was taken into care, and inevitably, things started to unravel at home, as what had happened was openly discussed amongst the family.

My relationship with my mum broke down: partly because she didn't initially believe my version of events, and partly because she said she was hurt that I hadn't confided in her. Needless to say, things were strained between us for some time, and I think the fact that she had stayed on with my father played a part in that.

I can't remember what got us talking again, but slowly the conversations came and the understanding started to work its way through. After a few major setbacks, I started to ask questions and find out more about what it had been like for my mother, when she'd found out what had happened between me and my father. She'd been running a small child-minding business at the time, which social services closed down. This had been her only source of income, so her financial independence and freedom were gone.

Continuing to live with my father, through the stigma and the whispers of relatives and people within the community who knew, couldn't have been easy for her. For obvious reasons she found it hard to talk about what my father had done to me; I could see that the thought of it pained and angered her too much. Yet, bit by bit, things slowly opened up, and I could see that we were no different from one another – we both wanted the same thing, we were just coming at it in very different ways.

One day, as I watched my stepsons and my son playing, I realized that at some point, later in their lives, they too could perhaps turn around and blame me for something I had or hadn't done – for not listening to them enough, for working too hard, for not spending enough quality time with them. In the case of my stepchildren – as hard as it is to write this, knowing I was only 19 years old at the time – they could even blame me for breaking up their parents' relationship and their family.

I also realized that I knew what it was like to be in a relationship that sucked the life out of you – one in which you lost all sense of your self and what that meant; one in which you stayed out of fear of the unknown, and for the sake of the children. In that moment I knew I needed to stop punishing my mother, for she was no different from me. I had to stop punishing her for not being the mum I thought she should have been, and for not loving me in the way I wanted and needed her to.

Also, for the way I felt she had rejected me, blamed me or was angry at me for what had happened between my father and me. It seemed as if in some way I was a constant reminder of the love, marriage, lifestyle and secure future I'd in some way 'stolen' from her – in 'allowing' my father's abuse to happen and not stopping it. This is something we've never talked about, but on some level I used to think it.

I instinctively knew that if I didn't start letting this go, and accept my mother and this situation for what it was, then any chance of repairing or rebuilding our relationship would be impossible. I'd become very good at telling myself I didn't care, when in truth I did.

So, instead of complaining that my mother never called me, I began to call her. Instead of moaning that she'd missed my birthday, I made a point of making hers special; and instead of longing to hear her say 'I love you', I started to say it to her at the end of our phone calls. Then, one day – after what felt like a lifetime of wanting – she ended our call with 'I love you, too'. It was quiet, gentle and unnatural, but she said it, and I could tell that she meant it. To this day, I've never told her how much I cried after I'd hung up. The irony was, though, that every time we'd spoken I'd already known it.

And today? Well, I'm the 'awful' child now – not that my mother would ever call me that. But she's always the one to call *me*: 'How are you, dear? Love you, miss you; let me know how you are?' She never openly complains about how long it's been since we last spoke, although she sometimes teases me by answering the call with 'Hello, stranger'. She no longer chastises me for not sending birthday gifts and cards, saying she'd rather see me than receive anything in the post. It's been a complete turnaround.

And so I've come to realize the power of acceptance, and how, by stepping into that space, it turned what felt like an almost hopeless situation into a very powerful transformation. Now I'm not suggesting that things will always be this way between us – I hope they will be, but nothing is fixed. But so far, our relationship has been going from strength to strength. So I believe that acceptance can move mountains and really help ease a lot of our internal suffering.

I often imagine how different our world would be – how many wars/ conflicts could potentially be avoided and communities transformed – if only we were all a little more accepting of ourselves and others.

QUESTION 2:
What do I accept?

> 'To be beautiful is to be yourself; you don't need to be accepted by others, you just need to accept yourself.'
> THICH NHAT HAHN

So Question 2 is all about acceptance – a very powerful space to be in and one that has really transformed my life! After experiencing my Wild Awakening turnaround with my mother, I knew that it was essential that I integrate acceptance into my daily life, as a part of my way of being. But what do I actually mean by acceptance?

I once thought that if I accepted something, that made it *acceptable* – and that's why I initially struggled with this Question. I knew that the way I'd been treated as a child, by both my parents, was not in the slightest sense acceptable; and I also knew that the way some of my partners had treated me, later in life, wasn't acceptable either. So I asked myself: *If I accept them and the situation, does that also mean I accept the way I was treated? Does that make it all right?* The answer to both questions is, of course, no, and ultimately it was never about the other person but about how I was failing to accept *myself*. But we'll come to that later.

So, with Question 2 firmly in place, out came my journal, and there began my responses, starting with the words 'I accept...' Here are some examples: *I accept that it will take me a while to get my head around this whole self-love thing. I accept that sometimes I'm fed up with feeling as if I'm constantly working on myself. I accept that my way of wanting to 'be' can be challenging for many of the men in my life. I accept that I'm not a 'systems' and 'follow-the-rules' person.*

Below are more examples of the powerful lessons and insights I've experienced since I started asking myself Question 2. As I share some of the Wild Awakenings that came up for me, feel free to consider whether introducing more acceptance into your life would benefit you right now.

And once again, remember that what follows is based simply on my personal experiences and on my *present* level of awareness, which is continuously deepening, expanding and growing. So please go with what works for you, and if you decide you want to challenge, skip, or stay open to anything that doesn't, feel free: it's your choice.

Acceptance is not giving up or giving in

I've learned that acceptance is not the same as resignation.

When I was with Mr Ex I believed that acceptance also meant some form of resignation. I was scared that if I accepted the mess I was in – and that I'd created it – nothing would ever change. It was as if, on some level, I was resigned to the fact that my life would always be that way: a sense of 'it is what it is'. And that felt awful – almost as if I were saying: 'I'm powerless to do anything about this.'

What I didn't realize at the time was that before I could change anything, I first needed to accept it – to see it for what it was. By not accepting my life for what it was, I was unconsciously fighting it, and as soon as you fight anything you've given your power away. It was then I realized that my fight and my need for things to be 'better' – something more than what they were – were causing the problem.

I slowly learned that until I accepted myself and 'what is', I would continue to attract unhealthy relationships. I learned that real acceptance is simply seeing things for what they are: no more, no less – and without judgment. It's from that place of honesty that we can start to create something new – something more aligned with what we really want.

I accept other people's ways of being

I've learned that true acceptance often requires us to suspend judgment, let go, and just 'go to bed'. We need to accept that we can't control other people's version of and response to 'what is' – we can only take responsibility for ourselves.

A while ago, a friend and I went away together for a few days. We had a great time until the last night, when we had a disagreement around a personal situation. In my usual way of wanting to know the answer/truth right away (my friend calls it 'interrogation', and I call it 'finding out what's really going on'!), I kept questioning him: *Why did you say that; what made you do that... but why?* Needless to say, after a while he became weary and defensive, and in turn, I felt frustrated that he wasn't being 'straight' with me. Then suddenly, mid-conversation, he announced that he was tired and was going to bed. Just like that!

'You can't leave me like this,' I cried. 'We haven't finished – I want to know *why.*' Instead of accepting that he was exhausted and needed some space to figure out what was going on for him internally, I was frustrated and really annoyed with him. Inside, I was shouting: *How can you sleep at a moment like this? We need to finish this, damn it!* (I was raised to believe that you should never go to bed on a bad word/argument – which is ironic when I think back to my childhood.)

So after he trotted off to bed, I stewed and paced, and washed the dishes to pretend I wasn't stewing. Then I pretended to be all Zen and calm, as if I'd let it all go. I clanged away at the sink, hoping the noise would eventually wake him up and that he'd be compelled to come back and finish our conversation (yeah, right). Anyway, a whole two hours later, I eventually went to bed. I was still fed up, still pretending I didn't care, but secretly hoping I hadn't pushed my friend too far in my relentless quest for the 'truth'.

At 5 a.m. I was still awake. I wanted a cuddle and I wanted to make sure my friend and I were still okay, so I crept down the hall to his room. I stood anxiously outside the door for 10 minutes, completely frozen, until I summoned up the courage to go inside. As I climbed into bed next to him, I could see he was fast asleep, clearly without a care in the world!

I wanted to strangle him and kiss him at the same time, for in that moment I 'got' it. *You idiot, Mary,* I thought: *what a waste of energy that was!* I laughed at how, despite all the 'work', and all the 'knowing', I'd once again pointlessly robbed myself of a peaceful moment, simply because I'd refused to accept 'what is' and let go of my need to know all the answers there and then. I snuggled under the duvet, exhausted, with a big smile on my face. As sleep came, I heard Mr Italy's voice laughing at me: 'Mary, you are such a disaster!' Aha – another Wild Awakening moment!

I can love myself just the way I am

I've learned that true acceptance is about letting go of my inner critic – my need to be 'perfect' – and loving myself just the way I am.

As I looked back at some of my relationships, I started to see some similar patterns in them. I realized that I'd wasted so much energy in trying to get other people to see me, love me, want me, hear me. It's just crazy! As well as punishing my mum for her shortcomings as a parent, I also punished Mr Ex – for not being 'the man I wanted him to be', and for the choice I made to stay with him, out of guilt, shame, and the desperate need for some security.

When I started to accept the reality of this, it was as if a weight had been lifted. I no longer needed to wear the mask of pretence. Acceptance allowed me to see that the only person I needed to accept was myself. Acceptance finally freed me up to ask myself, 'What do you *really* want, Mary?'

When I asked that question around my relationship at that time, with Mr Ex, I realized I just wanted to be happy – to experience real love, real life and real freedom. I realized I wanted to learn how to be there for 'me', to support myself. So, after 18 years with Mr Ex, acceptance had taught me the only thing I could control, or that mattered, was **my** life, **my** happiness and **my**self. As soon as I got that – although I was completely terrified and had no idea how I was going to support my son – I left the relationship.

Accepting myself has been and will continue to be an ongoing journey, with some really good days and moments and some totally disastrous ones. Flipping between downright painful and incredibly liberating! However, as time passes, and my confidence and connection to myself continue to grow, I notice that I'm becoming more comfortable in my own skin, and with my body.

And I know if I keep going, one day I'll be able to achieve one of my big self-love goals – loving myself enough to feel comfortable while wearing a swimming costume, in front of other people. So I can swim in the sea – *in the middle of the day* – and not feel ashamed of myself. To many people, this would seem like a small goal, but it's a massive one for me on my scale of self-love. I'm getting there!

I accept the 'light' and the 'dark'

*I've learned that we need to accept the **whole** of who we are, and that doing this not only has a personal impact, but a global one.*

I once read an interesting article by William Bloom that contained the following quote by Swiss psychotherapist Carl Jung: 'One does not become enlightened by imagining figures of light, but by making the darkness conscious.' I loved this, and taking Jung's insight one step further, I started to see how my overriding need to label things and divide them into 'good' and 'bad' was being mirrored in my world around me.

My father always told me that God had created me and brought me into his life so I could make him happy: that, apparently, was my purpose. It made me wonder whether, if certain people at the school I was attending had not struggled with the idea that my father, the 'good Christian man', could also be a man who abused his daughter, things could have turned out differently. It's a hard question to answer, and it shows us that one thing doesn't necessarily exclude another; someone can hold religious beliefs but also be an abuser – that's what happens when we become disconnected from ourselves.

Running with this idea, I then thought: *I wonder what this level of collective denial – this collective suppression and refusal to accept the parts of ourselves we don't want to see – would look like on a bigger scale: in communities, in countries, in large groups of people. What would our 'collective dark side' look like?*

The more I thought about it the more I realized that collective denial on that kind of scale could start wars, spark genocides, gather support for political parties or mass movements, allow people to be crushed because of their skin colour, their beliefs or their sexual orientation – it might even be powerful enough to destroy rainforests, melt icecaps and create dramatic changes in our environment. It could kill thousands, even millions, of people – in camps and detention centres, or openly, on the streets and in homes.

Many of us are shocked when we hear about the atrocities that are taking place in the world today; and we're all busy denying that they could ever happen to us or be committed by us – it would never happen in our town, our country, or in our homes. We blame it on mankind, others, the human race! But who is 'the human race' and who is 'mankind'? Aren't these just safe, hiding-out words for 'me'?

By not accepting that we *all* have the potential to become a murderer, a rapist or a racist – or that angry, violent person, or that bitter, sarcastic, manipulative, desperate to be seen, heard and loved person – we're failing to see the obvious happening right under our noses: happening all the time within us.

Would you kill someone in order to protect your child? Many would call that self-defence; others would call it murder: but who is right? Hang on, Mary, that's different, you cry. But is it really? How many times have we behaved in a way that was 'not us'? We are just as 'good' and as 'bad' as the people we read about, or see on the news, for there is no 'them and us'. There is *only* us, which means ultimately there is only an 'I' in this equation.

WILD AWAKENING WISDOM

- Accepting something doesn't mean that the situation or the person's behaviour itself is acceptable. It doesn't mean resignation, or that something is fixed or permanent. Acceptance can be very fluid and freeing: and it can open up infinite possibilities.

- We need to accept that we can't control other people's version of 'what is', or their response to it – we can only take responsibility for our own.

- Acceptance is about letting go of labels, judgment and unrealistic expectations of how others 'should' behave.

- Acceptance of self is the same as self-love: once we accept who we are, warts and all, we can really start to love who we are.

- I've learned that as soon as we accept that we have the potential and the capability to behave in exactly the same way as everyone else, and that there is no difference between 'us and them' – in fact, *there is no 'us and them'* – we have really understood and experienced the true meaning of unconditional love.

- Until we accept that we are all connected, we'll never really understand the power of our collective intention, in that when a large group with an aligned goal and clear purpose sets an intention, they can make the impossible, possible. Like collective prayer or meditation, this works both ways – irrespective of whether the goal is a positive or a destructive one.

Chapter 3

Fragile

'Spirituality means waking up. Most people...
[are] born asleep, they live asleep, they marry in
their sleep, they breed children in their sleep,
they die in their sleep without ever waking up.'

ANTHONY DE MELLO – *AWARENESS*

My father and I didn't really speak to each other once I left home. As the years went by, I stayed well away from him: I even missed the wedding of my first cousin – who was like a sister to me – as I was afraid of being in the same space as him.

I thought I'd made my peace with everything he'd done to me. I didn't believe I needed to forgive him – strangely, it didn't feel my place to do that – but I guess I'd just accepted it for what it was. However, I was aware that the memory of what had happened was still too charged to allow me to be anywhere near him. Also, being proud and stubborn, I didn't want him to see me during the low periods in my life – when I was overweight and clearly not happy. The thought of him judging me was too hard for me to bear.

So, when my older sister mentioned Dad during a phone call, exactly 13 years since I'd seen him last, I just froze. I think it ignited something in my body that was so strong, I actually zoned out of the rest of our conversation. All I could remember afterwards was the word 'cancer', and all I knew was that I couldn't have my father back in my life. I was sorry for him, truly I was – I wouldn't wish that disease on anyone – but it wasn't enough to want him back in my life.

Anyway, as the months passed, I didn't really hear much more about my dad or his illness; I think everyone knew it was best to stay clear of the subject around me. But then I had the call: Dad's condition had become much worse. He'd just come out of his second operation, to remove a large tumour in his brain, during which they'd discovered there was nothing more they could do for him. They'd called time, and if we wanted to see him, it had to be now.

Something in me said: *You need to go – you can't let it end this way, for his sake, as well as yours.*

I can't remember much about the car journey to the hospital that day; it's a bit of a blur. I can't recall whether my older sister was sitting next to me or whether she met me there. Two of my brothers joined us at the hospital; I remember continuously checking in on their ETA – knowing that I particularly needed my younger brother around: he was the one I'd found myself connecting with on an emotional level: we could talk.

We're a large family and while we're all very different, as a unit there are lots of little bonds between us, which at times bounce between different family members, depending on the situation and need. Age-wise, I'm sandwiched between two boys, and looking back I can see how, in their own different ways, they've pulled me out of a few holes during my life.

The older and slightly quieter one, who is in fact my middle brother, has always been there for me in a practical way – seeing things but not necessarily feeling the need to speak it all the time; he's such a generous soul. My younger brother, the more vocal one, is happy to pull up a chair and get stuck into the heart of the matter. Sometimes we'll become lost in conversation for hours, and he is

Fragile

my emotional support. I could see this was hard for him at times, as I was aware he really needed and wanted a father he could look up to – a strong male role model in his life; this is something he has said he still misses in so many ways today. I love my family.

When my dad fell ill, my younger brother pleaded with him to make amends with me, or at least write a letter of apology – anything to try and heal the pain he instinctively knew still existed inside of me and between the two of us. Sadly, my father refused to do so. He was probably too scared and too proud – who knows? There's one thing I know for sure, though – written proof of what he'd done to me was something my father could not have lived with.

After all, it had been the small note of apology he'd left after a particularly rough visit that had helped convince my mother that I wasn't lying about the abuse. My father usually got me to destroy these notes, but for some reason that time a voice persuaded me to take it out of the bin, tape it together and hold on to it. That was the last note he ever left. I don't know why my mother was persuaded by this 'evidence': perhaps it was because she knew it wasn't in my father's nature to write notes.

My younger brother recently told me that he remembers when the note came to light, and everyone found out what had been going on. He said he will never forget the way my dad went for me; grabbing the top of my head, as if he wanted to squash it. He said he had never seen such venom in someone's eyes. For the first time, he fronted my father, and threatened to kill him if he touched me again. It was hard for them all…

But my mother wasn't the only one who hadn't believed me at first: later I found out that one of the teachers I'd confided in at school had doubts about what I'd told him. Apparently, when he went to the headmaster (who was, ironically, a family friend) they were both unsure of the validity of my story. I think it was because I was so together, confident and happy on the outside, and they couldn't reconcile that with the things I'd revealed.

As we got closer to the hospital, I could suddenly feel the scared little girl coming back. Looking up at me with her big, terrified brown eyes, she was pleading with me to turn around. And even though I knew, rationally, that my father could no longer hurt me, I could feel the familiar anxiety rising. *It's not like he cares*, the little girl said. *He never said sorry, or made any attempts to make amends.* But something in me knew I needed to do this.

By the time we arrived, I was a mess – overly calm on the outside, but all pounding heartbeat and floods of adrenaline inside. I hated hospitals at the best of times – the plastic flooring, the harsh lighting, and the energy of death and disease: something no amount of disinfectant and alcoholic hand gels could hide. As we approached the door to Dad's room, I took a deep breath and then froze! I simply couldn't move past the doorway.

But then I thought: this is crazy – to come this far and then stop.

My sister squeezed past me, into the room, immediately disappearing to the side of Dad's bed. I could hear her weeping and calling his name, and I saw her hold his hands. But still I couldn't move. Luckily the room was L-shaped, with the bed positioned in such a way that I couldn't see his head or the top half of his body. The only part of him that was visible to me from my position in the doorway was his legs – hidden under the blue hospital blankets. To the bottom left of the bed was a chair and to the right of me was the bathroom door.

Mary, please, please I want to go home – now! the little girl in me cried. *Take me home: I don't want to be here!* I took a deep breath and calming her down, I scanned the room, trying to figure out the 'safest' place to be. The chair felt too close to the bed, too exposed; the doorway, where I stood, while too far away to see him, felt far enough away to protect myself. *Just go in and stop being silly*, I thought. *He's out of it – what are you scared of?*

As I watched my older sister, tears rolling down her face as she reflected on the loss and love of a father only a sweet, generous and forgiving heart like hers could hold, I knew I needed to move. Aiming for the safety of his feet, I took my first step into the room. And then I stopped. Suddenly, I couldn't breathe, see, or hear – my chest seemed to cave in. I needed a way out and I needed it now.

My body was on autopilot as I took a sharp turn right, opened the bathroom door and retreated inside, relieved to be away from his presence. Leaning against the wall, I slid to the floor, my thighs touching the coldness of the toilet basin. And then the dam burst. Not caring what was going on around me, I sobbed and sobbed and sobbed in a way that I never had before and never have since.

I cried for the little girl who had loved her father so much, and for the woman who loved him still, and for the lost soul who'd been searching for him in every relationship since – believing she wasn't worth more than what he'd left behind. I've no idea how long I sat there … half a minute, 30 minutes, an hour. The tears just kept coming, and as they fell to the ground so did the years of pain. Every part of me that had been holding this in finally just let go. And then suddenly, the tears stopped; as quickly as they had come they ceased.

To this day I can't explain it. Then I slowly stood up, took a deep breath, washed my face, straightened my jacket and opened the door as if nothing had happened. The only remaining memory was held in my body, as it gently sewed together the internal wounds.

'Are you okay?' my sister asked.

'Yes,' I replied, in a slightly rough, croaky voice.

As I successfully made my way to the end of the bed – my heart beating louder than any machine on the ward – his top half came into sight. He was barely recognizable: his face hardly visible, his eyes closed, his head bandaged, and his body so still. All I could think was: he is so much smaller than I remember. The man who'd towered over me, terrified me with his hands, his words, his body, was now so small, bent and twisted. I studied the way my sister held his aged hand, stroking his arm, rocking and weeping – the thought of being near his naked flesh made my stomach turn.

I stayed at his feet – which were safe, hidden as they were under layers of blankets. I tried to touch them; my hand hovered, but I couldn't lower it. The little girl pulled me backwards, whispering, *No, Mary, the blankets aren't thick enough to protect us.* For once she was right.

Suddenly, one of the nurses came to the door, and the next thing I knew, my sister had disappeared and it was just the two of us. I don't know what part of me took over, but I gently started sidestepping to the middle of the bed. I looked up at his head, seeing nothing and in some way feeling nothing, except that my father had had enough. It felt as if the guilt was literally eating him alive – his body at dis-ease with its 'self'; as if it struggled to erase the energetic imprint of what had happened.

And while I couldn't know for sure, I felt as if I hadn't been the only one who had suffered. Staring at his fragile frame I knew there was only one thing left to do. It was time to let him go – to set us both free and openly make peace. So, with that as my sole thought and purpose, I leaned over him, closed my eyes and whispered the first thing that came to me: 'Dad, it's okay. I'm fine; I don't hate you, I promise. You can go now, it's fine… everything is fine. I promise.'

To this day I can't remember if I told him I loved him, or that I forgave him – it almost didn't feel my place or my right to forgive. I don't know – it felt as if the only forgiveness needed was between him and his self. As for loving him, in some way I knew that he knew I did, or at least I hoped he did.

My sister returned to the room, and not long afterwards, my brothers arrived. Amid our sombre greetings and a concerned 'are you okay?' hug from my younger brother, I started to retreat, almost feeling as if I didn't belong there. And the truth was that in some ways I didn't, for my father and I hadn't spoken for more than a decade.

As I stood outside the room, waiting for the consultant, my mind wandered back to the time I felt I knew the man dying in the bed. To the time when we were both happy to pay the price of our warped and twisted relationship (me as a desperate little girl who let her body be used in return for any type of love; and my father as the thief who stole my most sacred gift – the one that I should have been allowed to hold on to until I *chose* to share it; the one that should *never* be taken by a father, a protector.

I remembered the time we'd sat in his car, with the sun shining in through the windows, and he'd told me about the hopes he'd had as a teenager. How he'd always dreamed of running away with a 'special person' who would become the love of his life. In that moment, as he spoke, he was no longer a father, burdened by responsibilities, bills, a family he was sometimes struggling to connect with; he didn't have to go to work, to play the game. He was a teenager once more, still talking of running away – but with me, his 13-year-old daughter.

With every cell in my body sighing, I knew it was time to let go – to release the pain of the child, the loss, the sadness, the shame and the guilt. As I headed back to the room I really 'got' how fragile we are, and I also knew it was time to let go of a father I'd never really had.

QUESTION 3:
What do I want to let go of?

> 'Some of us think holding on makes us
> strong, but sometimes it is letting go.'
> HERMAN HESSE

So Question 3 is all about letting go. This is something we talk about needing to do more often. We recognize the benefits of it, but it's something very few of us, including myself, really know how to do at a deeper, core level.

This realization really hit me after I visited my father in hospital before he died. What I believed was 'letting go' turned out to be suppression, burying the past deep down inside where no one could reach it, including myself. I became aware of how, in holding on to false beliefs and not facing things fully, I was actually creating bigger blocks in my life – emotionally, physically and within many of the relationships I'd been attracting.

As soon as I became aware of how much I'd been holding on to, I knew I needed to ask the question 'What do I want to let go of?' So what *do* I want to let go of? My goodness, this Question has always been so easy to answer! I'll always start my response with the words 'I let go of...' even if I haven't *yet* let go of whatever it is I want to let go of! I'll start the answer this way, because it's something *I know I want to do*. For example, I know my excess weight still serves as some form of protection for me, so I often write things like: *I let go of whatever I feel my body needs protecting from. I let go of the guilt and shame I may still be carrying as a result of my childhood and my past relationships. I let go of feeling unattractive and believing that I need to lose weight before I am acceptable.*

So, in this way, the answer to Question 3 can almost be an *invitation* to start letting go of things. Below are some of the powerful lessons and insights I've discovered or experienced on a deeper level since I started asking myself this question. As you read through them, if anything comes up for you feel free to make a note of it, and when you start to work through the 9 Questions yourself, which I'll show you how to do in Part III, you can explore it further.

And remember: what follows is based simply on my personal experiences and on my *present* level of awareness, which is continuously deepening, expanding and growing. So please go with what works for you, and if you decide to challenge, skip, or stay open to anything that doesn't, then feel free: it's your choice.

Letting go is like a deep cleansing of the soul

I've learned, and personally experienced, that everything in life is made of energy – basically, everything we know to be real, even our thoughts and emotions, is one big sexy ball of energy. So as soon as we hold on to something that isn't needed or isn't serving us, it can create huge energy blocks that often lead to some form of dis-ease.

Letting go of something that's weighing us down or holding us back can be so liberating. Mentally and physically, it removes unnecessary 'energy blocks' in our system, often leaving us feeling lighter and more energized. However, if these energy blocks are held onto or left unnoticed for too long, they often become toxic and start to show up in the body on a physical level, often as ailments, or as stress or dis-ease, and can sometimes prove fatal. Louise Hay's book *You Can Heal Your Life* and Caroline Myss's *Anatomy of the Spirit* are great introductions to these issues (I talk about these books further in Part III.)

So, when I talk here about letting go, I don't just mean the small, day-to-day things. I'm also referring to things at the deeper, almost core/soul level – which, if left unaddressed, will call for our full attention at some point; they will call for our total surrender to the lesson life is asking us to 'get'. And by that stage, the lesson might not be so gentle in letting us know it's there!

Sometimes, life calls for complete surrender

*I've learned that sometimes the hardest part of letting go is simply **deciding** to let go: the second we do it we often realize that the result is not half as bad as we thought it would be. Life is inherently designed to support us at all times, and be there for us. Which makes sense if you believe that **we are life**.*

Letting go tends to be focused on giving up something that's no longer serving us, making us happy, or allowing us to feel at peace and connected with who we are and where we want to be in our lives. But I've also come to realize that life itself is all about letting go: we often talk about being on 'a journey' to knowing ourselves, as if there's a big destination we need to reach. However, what I've learned is that there is nowhere to get *to* – instead, the journey is simply about letting go of anything and everything that's stopping us from fully 'knowing ourselves'.

Letting go of the bigger, deeper stuff can be really hard. Sometimes it can feel as if we've been hit from nowhere, as we experience a deep pain around an old memory or something we really thought we were over. I call this the 'growing pains of the soul', where our soul, or the real part of us, our authentic self, wants us to grow beyond the place we're currently at in life. This often requires us to leave behind some of the masks we use to protect ourselves, or to 'get real' around what we really want out of life and who we really want to be.

Sometimes this process is so intense that it can feel as if everything we know in our lives to be true – everything we relied on, got security and comfort from, or even based our identity on – starts to crumble around us, potentially resulting in a significant change in our home environment, our lifestyle, our personal relationships, our relationship with money, our work, our health, the way we see ourselves, our identity and so on.

This is something I'm currently going through on all levels, and while some of my friends are calling it a midlife crisis, I like to call it a midlife realization: where you know that you no longer fit the life you've been living. And although it requires a great deal of courage, honesty, and trust – especially when the 'what next' looks so daunting and uncertain – simply making the decision to let go, no matter how hard it might seem at the time, can be incredibly liberating. It allows you to uncover the next part of yourself, often organically moving things forward with ease.

Letting go can take place in stages

*I've learned that letting go can happen in waves and layers
– triggering different things at different times. Certain
themes reoccur in our lives, but that doesn't mean we
are not growing or letting go: it can simply mean we're
experiencing the lesson on a deeper layer, allowing us to
uncover and discover more and more about ourselves.*

When we let go of something, much of what we then experience tends to happen at a surface level: there might be some pain or discomfort at the outset, but over time things do get easier. Life goes on, and eventually we regain our 'back to normal' stride. But then we might face another trigger: either from the same person or from a similar event or situation.

This is what happened to me with my father. I was convinced that I'd let go of so much of my childhood stuff, and on some level I *had* found a way of coping with it all. I genuinely believed that, because I was no longer having the dreams, the flashbacks, the constant anxiety or the irrational anger, I had let go.

However, I had no idea of the true impact of my messed-up childhood and prolonged abuse at a core level. I couldn't see the deeper effect it was having on my decision-making process; I didn't realize it was making me hold myself back and settle for less, based on where my self-worth and self-love were at any given time. I was unable to see the glaring signs that I hadn't truly let go: my weight, my relationship, my work, how I felt about myself. All around me, everything was shouting that things were clearly *not* working.

It wasn't until I left Mr Ex, and had some physical space, that I could start to look at what was *really* going on beneath the surface. It was then I realized that letting go can happen in waves and layers. By layers, I mean like the layers of an onion. As each layer of pain or hurt – or a realization – is uncovered, we see another side of the way our past experiences are manifesting and playing out in our lives – especially around the decisions and choices we are constantly making.

And by waves, I mean the way our emotions and feelings can come and go, like the waves of the ocean. Sometimes the intensity around what's buried can feel overwhelming, almost knocking us off our feet and wiping us out, and other times it is more soft and gentle, manageable, bearable – we know they are there but we can function. The beauty with waves is that as long as we stay open and aware, each wave – as well as bringing some new insights and lessons – is also an opportunity to let something else go, to let it get washed away and recycled by Mother Nature. Until, over time, they get a little softer and a little gentler until the pain is no longer there.

The process of letting go can't be forced

I've learned that no matter how hard or painful the process of letting go might become, forcing ourselves to hurry it may cause more harm than good, and potentially drive the issues deeper.

I will never forget the time Alternatives hosted a workshop called 'Awakening your Menstrual Power', which was fronted by two incredible women – Alexandra Pope and Sjanie Hugo Wurlitzer. (I've since told Alexandra and Sjanie this story, so I know they won't mind what comes next!) Initially, I found the title of the workshop quite alarming, and I thought to myself: *Good grief, who on earth will go to that?*

Usually, I wouldn't have been seen dead attending such a thing myself! (I'd been brought up to suffer in silence when it came to menstruation, so this sounded way too in-your-face, 'red tent hippie-ish' for me.) However, within 10 minutes of it starting, I was hooked, and at the end, I left convinced that every woman and teenage girl should attend events like this one. It not only changed the way I viewed my monthly cycle, it also showed me how so many aspects of my personality, and the way I was living my life, were actually changing my body's natural rhythm, and my physiology.

I discovered that I'm someone who naturally fast-tracks most things in life, including letting go. My idea of effectively letting go of something was to have a logical conversation with myself around the area of challenge, and then to allow myself anywhere between two hours and a day to wallow or feel sorry for myself before I 'got on with things'.

After my long-term relationship broke down, I even fast-tracked my emotional release. I'd listen to loads of melancholy music, then watch *Into the Wild* (one of my favourite films), followed by episodes of *Grey's Anatomy*. All of which usually induced a temporary state of depression and tears, and then I'd snap myself out of it – telling myself to get on with life and stop wasting time.

Over the course of Alexandra and Sjanie's workshop I learned that the different stages of a woman's cycle are like the seasons – each one serving its own purpose. When I tracked 'my seasons', I wasn't surprised to learn that I was rushing through my 'autumn, winter' (the body's downtime; its reflective, inward period) and then spending ages in my 'spring, summer' (the creative and 'doing' phase).

By failing properly to honour my downtime, I was failing to honour and care for the whole of me. And then it hit me: it was as if, without even realizing it, I was telling myself I didn't deserve or wasn't worthy of taking that time out for myself. I could really see that my struggle with self-worth and self-love – a huge, ongoing learning in my life – was showing up everywhere.

It's actually only recently that I've started to really acknowledge how deep it all goes, and to slow down and take slightly better care of myself. This is a biggie for me, and one I will continuously be working on. Anyway, I have to say that the workshop blew me away, so well done, ladies!

Letting go doesn't always have to be EPIC

I've learned that letting go can sometimes come really easily. We may not need to spend a day at a workshop, beating cushions, or six months in an ashram in India, or to throw plates out of our kitchen window, or to write a heartfelt, 10-page letter to someone we only dated for a month. It may be as simple as just 'getting' it: seeing the lesson for what it is, letting it go and moving on.

We often imagine that letting go of something big will involve scaling a mountain of pain and tears, but sometimes it can be really easy and quite simple. Sometimes a subtle shift in perspective can open up a whole new horizon. Have you noticed how great children are at letting go? They can be at each other's throats one minute, and best friends the next, carrying on as if nothing has happened.

I've yet to hear a small child say: 'You know what, two weeks ago, when I was getting out of bed, just before breakfast, you hit me… and then the day after, just before bath time, after you took my foam shapes, you did it again. You know, that didn't feel good and I'm still struggling to deal with it and let it go today!' Children live in the moment – pure live streaming – and it is brilliant! That is real life, real presence. And we were once that way ourselves.

WILD AWAKENING WISDOM

- I've learned that sometimes we can bury things so deeply, the things we are holding on to literally show up in our bodies. So to really let go of something, we need to be aware that we might have to deal with it on three levels: the mind (our thoughts), the body (physical) and the soul (our core).

- Letting go can happen in stages – in waves and layers – so don't be alarmed if the same thing comes around again and again on a deeper, more profound level.

- We can't force, or fast-track, the process of letting go. Sometimes time, space and being patient – allowing nature's natural cycle of release and flow – may be the only thing that's needed.

- Letting go doesn't always have to be dramatic – sometimes a good rest or a walk in natural surroundings can bring an entirely new perspective.

- Letting go is rarely about the other person, or the 'thing' that happened to us – it's usually about something deeper going on inside us that the other person/thing is triggering, or shining a light on.

Chapter 4
Thank You

*'God is a metaphor for that which transcends all
levels of intellectual thought. It's as simple as that.'*
JOSEPH CAMPBELL

Now, if the following concept is new to you, go with me on this
one before you freak out. What would you say if I told you that we
actually get to write the story of our life? (Still with me? Gentle lead
in…) That we get to choose the life themes, or life lessons, we want
to experience, and we get to choose the people (the family) we
want to be born into. So for me, being born into the family of my
biological parents, and knowing the type of parents they would be
and what I would experience as a child, was actually my pre-birth
conscious choice. (Are you still with me?!)

I say *pre-birth conscious choice*, as the moment I was born I had
no conscious memory of it being my choice. But what would you
say if I told you that I chose everything that happened to me as a
child – my biological parents, my foster parents, the abuse, moving
around, my challenging relationships in adulthood; all the pain, the
joy, the highs, the lows and so on? How would you react if I said
that, on some level, I asked for and chose the life I was born into,
before I was even born?

What I've just described is the concept of 'soul contracts' (lesson plans or agreements we make as pre-birth conscious choices, and which we then follow as our path through life). I found this difficult to grasp at first, and to help me get my head around it, I likened it to a simulation game.

When I was younger, I loved *Star Trek* – a series Stoner Zen had introduced me to – and on board the *Starship Enterprise*, there was a simulator room in which a crew member could choose the theme, character, setting etc. of whatever it was they wanted to experience, and also decide how long they wanted it to last. The person in the simulator sometimes got so carried away with their experience they forgot that they had created it in the first place.

Something similar happens to the people who take part in TV reality shows, as the audience watches their antics, sometimes in horror, thinking: *Why would they want to do that on TV? Don't they realize that millions of people are watching?* But, as human beings, we can soon get sucked into the reality playing out in front of us; lots of the contestants on these shows say afterwards that after a while, they forgot the cameras were there.

Sometimes I see a soul contract as resembling a simulation game in which we get to choose everything. For example if, pre-birth, we've chosen to learn about self-love in a particular way, we choose our parents, the setting, everything – but the way life is mapped out is a bit like the levels of a computer game; we need to complete a certain level – collecting things (lessons) along the way before we can open up the gateway to the next level (which also has challenges and rewards we need to experience and collect along the way). And so on.

So that's how I see a soul contract: we are in this life, forgetting that the cameras we set up are there. And in some other place within us – but greater than our physical body – we are watching ourselves; in my case, sometimes in horror!

Now for those of you who are hearing about the idea of soul contracts for the first time, it might sound crazy. When I first heard about it, I thought so too. I mean, I had an awareness of it, and I used to think it was what people meant when they spoke about 'fate' and 'karma'. But I didn't give it much thought or attention; and I definitely didn't believe I had *chosen* to be sexually abused as a child!

But then one day I watched a documentary called *The Unmistaken Child*, which explores the Buddhist concept of reincarnation and follows the four-year search for the reincarnation of the late, world-renowned Tibetan master Lama Konchog. It's a beautiful documentary that takes the viewer through the breathtaking scenery of Nepal (a sad reminder of the way the country looked before the tragic 2015 earthquake, which took so many lives and homes).

The film really made me question why I am here, and why I would have chosen this life. Coming from a Christian background I initially found the Buddhist concept of reincarnation difficult to grasp, but it fascinated me and in a strange way, it also resonated with me. The more I looked into it, the more the concept of soul contracts kept popping up.

Then I came across Dan Millman's aforementioned book, *The Life You Were Born to Live*, in which he explains that the date of our birth is not just some random numbers; in fact, they have a hidden meaning which, when added together in a certain way, reveals the challenges and tests we have chosen to go through in life in order eventually to realize our life purpose – what we are here to do. Millman constantly reminds us, though, that this 'rarely comes easy'.

Well, when I read about my numbers (29/11), what I discovered about myself was so accurate, it changed my entire way of thinking about my life – the things that had happened to me as a child; why I'm here; and why I'm convinced that our soul's purpose is simply to know ourselves, nothing else.

I've also recently discovered Caroline Myss's book *Sacred Contracts*, in which she says that our 'lack of self-understanding and direction is a health problem itself, for it can lead to all sorts of emotional stress, including depression, anxiety, and fatigue, and eventually illness...' She then goes on to talk about how it is not just our minds that need to know our life purpose and mission – our body and our spirit do too. It's a truly insightful read, and one I would highly recommend.

Anyway, all of this started me thinking. What if, before I was born, my soul got to choose what it would like to experience here on Earth, and to define its purpose? What if my soul got to decide which lessons I would like to learn, the type of family I would like to be born into, and specific things I would like to experience?

Perhaps I'd even call in a few old souls to come and help me through some of my experiences – the people we call soulmates: those we know so well it is as if we've lived a whole other life with them. (This is something I've experienced very powerfully with Mr Italy. It's a bit like a déjà vu feeling or a really deep knowing.)

Now, as I said before, I'm far from being an expert on this topic, and if you'd told me all of this a few years ago I would have reacted angrily: what about all the people around the world – especially the women and children – who are being tortured, raped, or experiencing the most hideous things at the hands of their fellow human beings? Why would *anyone* want that or choose that? But now I realize this is the human part of me reacting: the part that still separates things into 'good' and 'bad' – the unconscious part that has no memory of a soul contract being made.

The 'knowing' part of me (my soul) does not and cannot differentiate between good and bad, right and wrong; it can only see the gift and perfection in everything that is unfolding in my life – knowing that everything is perfect and as it should be. And is ultimately here to allow me to learn the lessons I came to learn, so my soul can grow.

Everything we are seeing and experiencing around us is not only a reflection of the internal journey we've chosen to walk, but also a school for us to learn about ourselves. It's a classroom in which each experience we have, each person we meet, every decision we make, and every thought we allow in is a lesson, designed to help us study for one single test – one that many of us are unaware we are sitting every single second of our lives. It's the test of 'knowing who we are': not on a human level, but on a deep, soul level; and when we get that, we've 'got' the purpose of life.

That's when the real fun begins, and that is why I'm deeply grateful.

QUESTION 4:
What am I truly, deeply grateful for?

> 'If the only prayer you said in your life was
> "thank you", that would suffice.'
>
> MEISTER ECKHART

Question 4 is something I have always been connected to, even before the moment on the bridge. But the *deep* element of being grateful was actually a recent addition, something I explain below.

We're all familiar with how good it feels when someone tells us they are grateful for us. When someone we really care about says this in a genuine way, it can move us very deeply, and warm us up from the inside out. Well, imagine that feeling multiplied a hundredfold, for no reason other than the fact that we are alive and connected to what life is all about. We feel so grateful to be here – truly grateful to be alive and to experience this complete and utter peace and bliss. That moment, right there, is what I call deep gratitude; it's when it gets us on every level.

But it was only when I learned more about the concepts I have described above that I was able to experience deep gratitude. I'm finding that the more connected I am to the present moment, the more natural this state of deep gratitude becomes. So Question 4 is all about being deeply grateful and I love it.

So with Question 4 firmly in place, out came my journal and I started to write: 'What am I truly, deeply grateful for?' The answers just flowed: *I am truly, deeply grateful that I've had the privilege of experiencing what it means to be a mother. I am truly, deeply grateful that I've had the chance to experience the reflection of the love my soul is in the eyes of another person. I am truly, deeply grateful that I have this newfound awareness around my life and what it means to be alive.*

I've found that the deeper effects of being really grateful are very powerful, and when I introduced this form of gratitude into my life on a more regular basis it started to transform the way I saw myself, the people in my life and my world around me. I became a deep joy magnet, thankful and truly grateful for the soul's journey I'd chosen. I love it!

So, as I share some of the answers and Awakenings that came up for me as I sat and answered Question 4, feel free to think about what you are personally grateful for right now, and make a note of where you feel that in your body – is it just a thought or can you really *feel* deep gratitude in your body?

If you have any Wild Awakenings – or 'aha' moments – while doing this, make a note of them, and when you start to work through the 9 Questions yourself, which I'll show you how to do in Part III, you can explore what came up for you. First, a quick reminder that what follows is based simply on my personal experiences and on my *present* level of awareness, which is continuously deepening, expanding and growing. So please go with what works for you, and if you decide to challenge, skip, or stay open to anything that doesn't, then feel free: it's your choice.

Deep gratitude is a form of meditation

I've learned that deep gratitude is as powerful as meditation, because the only way we can really experience it is when we're fully connected to and in the present moment. Deep gratitude is a way of being.

In recent years there have been a lot of studies about the benefits of being grateful, and it's thought that keeping a simple gratitude journal can transform the way we approach our day, improve our levels of happiness and our lives in general. It's something that costs nothing but is so rewarding, and while it's easy at what I call the 'surface level' to recognize the things, people and moments we are grateful for in our lives, it's so easy to forget what that looks like on a day-to-day basis – something I've too often learned the hard way.

When I first started to keep a gratitude journal, it read like a shopping list of people and things I liked. It was very disconnected and it reminded me of how, when we were young, my brothers and sisters and I used to see how quickly we could say grace, almost without breathing – 'Thank you for our food Amen!' – just so we could tuck into our meal. I mean, we couldn't have got it any shorter!

Over time, as I've observed myself and others, I've noticed that most of us don't really stop and connect to what it means to be truly grateful. We say 'thank you' without making any eye contact with the person we're thanking, or showing any form of genuine appreciation; we do it just because we've been 'taught' to say thank you. It's a bit like our nice, polite and meaningless greetings. We Brits do politeness rather well – something Mandena and Mr Italy constantly tease me about.

However, what I'm coming to realize is that deep gratitude requires us to be fully connected to the moment – to be present, simply to be. Whenever we experience a strong sense of gratitude we're experiencing life itself – not our to-do list, our mental chatter or our worries about something that happened in the past or may happen in the future – just pure life. So one could say that deep gratitude is a form of meditation.

I accept and let go of regret

I've learned that focusing on what I'm grateful for has not only transformed the way I experience my day, it has stopped me from wishing my life away.

Regret is when you can't let that 'if only' thought go; regret is when you wish you could go back; regret is when you're judging the outcome you had. Regret is continuously looking back on things and wishing they had been better or different. Often, when I'm looking at old photos of my younger self, I'll find myself wishing that I still looked that way – even though, at the time the photo was taken, I actually hated my body and felt fat.

In moments of pure gratitude, when I'm really connected to how amazing we are as human beings, I realize how many years I've spent wishing my life away. Wishing I were slimmer, in a better relationship, that I had more time, or lived in a warmer climate. My goodness, the list goes on and on. If I ask myself why I was doing this, the answer is simple: because I was being ungrateful.

I realized that regret is just another form of disconnection – it's a sign that we're shut off from what's happening in the present, that we've become lost in our mind, in old memories. A lack of gratitude is not only a sign of disconnection from self, it's an inability to love and accept ourselves/the situation, because the amount of self-love we have directly correlates to how connected we are with ourselves. And therefore, because I was disconnected and unable to feel gratitude and appreciation for myself – basically, love for myself in that moment – I attracted people/mirrors who didn't appreciate me either.

Just think about it: if I'd appreciated my body in the moment I was experiencing my body, that moment in time would have been very different for me. I would have seen what a beautiful body I had in that moment; I would have been truly, deeply grateful for what my body was allowing me to do. I would have treasured it, looked after it better, treated it like the temple to the soul that it is (something I'm still struggling with today... I'm getting there, but it's still hard).

So alongside listening to music and being in nature, I have found that deep gratitude is one of the quickest and most powerful ways of taking me out of my head – stopping me from wishing away my life, and bringing me back into the moment.

I want to show the people who matter, that they matter

I've learned that gratitude can bring many hidden gifts. If we stay open to these, they can surprise us in so many ways. I've also learned that it's all too easy to take things for granted – sometimes we only really appreciate what we have once it's gone, or when we are about to lose it.

I love gratitude – when I feel my heart expand and I experience that immense, overwhelming appreciation and total connection to the moment; when I'm so thankful for the lessons I've learned, the space I'm in and the people in my life. I'm constantly telling people how much I love them, and how blessed and fortunate I am to be alive.

While I often feel this level of gratitude, I've also noticed how easy it is to let it slip, to become disconnected and to start to take those moments and people for granted. For example, despite my *telling* people how much they mean to me, the level of contact I had with my friends and family was often saying something different.

I found I was constantly hiding behind excuses: *I'm rubbish at birthdays and things like that. You know me by now – I'm sorry, I will get better.* And while I still don't believe in buying presents for the sake of it, or celebrating things just because of a date in the diary, I'm slowly getting to show at least, in small ways, that I'm very grateful to have those people in my life.

So, for example, when I couldn't get over to my foster sister's place very often, due to work commitments and the distance involved, I would call her for a chat or text her – sending her little messages and updates, letting her know I was thinking of her until we next met up. And these are memories and conversations that will stay with me forever. So any day or moment can be a celebration: it's simply about the connection, coming together, and expressing gratitude from a real space.

Deep gratitude removes judgment

I've learned to be grateful for everything that happens in life, 'good' or 'bad', because when we move to a space of deep gratitude we realize there is no good or bad, there is only life.

My foster sister has recently been diagnosed with stomach cancer, and I've been shocked at how quickly the disease has taken over her body; I'm also in complete awe of how she has handled it. As soon as the family heard about her illness, we all started to visit her more often, and while I haven't been able to see her as frequently as I would have liked, I've noticed that the time we've spent together has transformed our relationship.

I've learned a lot more about our childhood, growing up, etc., and we discovered that we actually have a great deal more in common than we realized. Apparently, her grandfather had been massively into gardening and growing his own food, and she too is fascinated by medicinal plants and had an allotment for years. Well, this tapped into my newfound love for permaculture, so we swapped stories. She gave me books and tips and I showed her the pictures of my trip to Italy, and my juicy permaculture teacher (she advised me to stay well clear, as he had trouble written all over him!) We've spent a lot of time laughing.

One day, though, as I walked around her huge garden, I felt a pang of sadness that it had taken something like this to bring us back together. I have no idea how my sister's illness has impacted on her children, and right now I really feel for them, but from my own perspective, it seems that, sometimes, it takes big things like this – trigger events as I call them – to get us to wake up; to help us step into a more open, real and connected space within ourselves and with others.

My sister's illness has kicked our relationship into a more real space, with a deeper, more genuine appreciation and connection for and to each other. The chats we've had about our lives, and the things we've been through, have become more real. For the first time I told her about my childhood, the abuse I'd suffered when I went back to my birth parents; and she opened up about her life. We recognized that we'd both experienced similar pains, and could relate to so many of the decisions and choices we'd made subsequently as a result of that.

In some unspoken way I could see that we were both deeply grateful for the individual gifts our time together had given us. So let's not wait until moments like this before we get real in our lives. I've learned that, rather than get angry or see it as something 'bad', it's important to seize the gift that is being offered. (Thank you for sharing your gift with me, sis xx.)

WILD AWAKENING WISDOM

- I've learned that living from a space of deep gratitude is a much easier and much more natural way of being than we realize.

- Sometimes, it's only when times are dark that we can really see and appreciate the bright stars – the amazing people who light up our life.

- I've learned that focusing on what we're grateful for can transform the way we experience our day.

- When it's understood and experienced on a deeper level, gratitude can be as powerful as meditation. It's an amazing way of bringing us back to the present moment.

- When we are in a space of gratitude it's hard to judge things as good or bad: judgment ceases to exist, simply because appreciation can only see through the eyes of love.

Chapter 5

It's My Life

*'If we do not know what port we are
steering for, no wind is favourable.'*
SENECA

Back when vision boards – those collages containing images and affirmations that represent our dreams, goals, and things that make us happy – were all the rage, I saw a woman on *The Oprah Winfrey Show* talk about hers; I'll never forget the way she went through all the things she'd attracted into her life as a result of creating the board. Everyone on the show was so impressed, ooh-ing and aah-ing, and I thought to myself, *How cool, I'm going to make myself one of those!*

So I went about creating my vision board: sourcing all the ingredients for my 'ideal life' from overpriced magazines and inspirational handouts. The problem was, no matter how hard I tried, my board just didn't work: things kept dropping off it, and the content never felt quite right. I meditated on what I wanted to receive; I cut out loads of dramatic 'think big' pictures; I even bought a fake one-million-pound note, which I photocopied (I was on a budget), carrying one copy around in my purse and *supergluing* the original to my board – I wasn't going to let that fall off: I wanted to be rich, damn it!

But the colours of the pictures on my vision board faded, and their corners curled in the sun, and my bank balance remained the same. I thought it must be a sign I was going to be financially up and down forever! I was doubly gutted when I found out I could have bought a fake one-*billion*-pound note! *What the hell?* I thought – annoyed that I was clearly still playing it small! And then one day, I came home to find my vision board on the floor, wedged behind a set of drawers. It looked lost and pathetic, as if it were begging me to put it out of its misery. It looked as if I was never going to manifest the life of my dreams.

Finally, as a last resort, I bought a book about how to create a successful vision board, and as I flicked through the images of other people's successful vision boards, two things really hit me: a) they all looked pretty much the same, with pictures of big houses, fast cars, wedding rings, babies, hot-looking men or women; there were one or two creative and personal things, but overall the content was similar, and b) while all of the boards represented what these people wanted to attract into their lives, there were no examples of what they were willing to do to achieve it – what they were willing to put back out into the world. So the energy felt stuck, as if it didn't flow.

You see, I've realized I'm a big believer in the idea that life rewards us for what we put into it, and that how we choose to spend our time should be driven by what we love, not what we believe we'll gain from it materialistically. I believe in being of service to the world, and while I have no issue with the desire for financial security, I think it's important that it's combined with being of service.

Looking back on this time, I can see that the true meaning of manifestation, and the real essence of the Law of Attraction (the concept that our mode of thinking directly affects what the Universe gives us), got distorted. It ended up becoming a big excuse to endorse the accumulation of more stuff, creating empty fulfilment behaviour and an accompanying mindset.

And the more I saw of this, the more it turned me off. One day I sat down and asked myself: Mary, what is it that you really, really want to invite into your life? What do you want to experience, and how do you want to experience it? What's underneath this desire to 'have things' – and what gap is it trying to fill? What are you willing to put back into the world? Where do you want to be of service? The more I sat with these questions the more I started to realize that what I *thought* I wanted was nowhere near what I *really* wanted.

And that's when I had my Wild Awakening around *true* manifestation. The problem was, I was so disconnected from myself that even if I'd manifested everything on the vision board it would probably have disappeared pretty quickly. I was so blocked, I was unable to receive or fully appreciate who I was, let alone what I had.

Everything we manifest and attract into our lives is there for one reason – to enable us to grow and know ourselves on a deeper level, a soul level. Real manifestation can only operate on a soul level, and only when we're connected to that space within – the authentic core of who we are – can we truly understand what it means to live an abundant life.

In the end, everything we need is already right in front of us. In fact, it's actually *within* us – and so the closer we get to knowing ourselves, and realizing who we are, the closer we get to experiencing what true manifestation is all about. The truth of it is, if we truly 'got' how magnificent we are, we would never worry about anything.

QUESTION 5:
What do I really want to invite into my life?

*'Of all the liars in the world, sometimes
the worst are your fears.'*
RUDYARD KIPLING

So I found my fifth Question – and it's all about what we want to invite into our lives. What we want to experience, manifest or create – what we *really* want. This has been an interesting one for me as I've recently seen that my levels of manifestation are directly linked to how much I trust myself and trust life.

Working through this question has really helped me see that when I'm in a trusting space, and know what I want, I manifest immediately – and I mean *immediately* – and when I'm disconnected, unsure of what I want and no longer trusting myself, everything becomes murky.

With Question 5 firmly in place out came my journal, and there began my answers, starting with the words 'I invite…' Here are some that have come to me recently: *I invite more space for myself, improved health, and more fun! I invite real relationships and connections: with friends, family members and on an intimate level. I invite shitloads of money and connections so I can make all my dream projects a reality!*

Below are some of the powerful lessons and insights I've discovered or experienced on a deeper level since I started asking myself Question 5. As I share what came up for me, feel free to think about what you want to invite into your life, right now. What is it that you *really* want – and what would that look like right now? If you have any Wild Awakenings – 'aha' moments – while doing this, make a note of them, and when you start to work through the 9 Questions yourself, you can explore what came up for you.

And remember: what follows is based simply on my personal experiences and on my *present* level of awareness, which is continuously deepening, expanding and growing. If you decide you want to challenge, skip, or stay open to anything that doesn't work for you, then feel free: it's your choice.

I need to check life's invitations before accepting them

I've learned that life is continuously sending us invitations, gently asking us what it is that we really want.

Sometimes in life it can feel as if we're sitting on the sidelines at a ball with our dance card in our hand, waiting for our next dance partner – or in this case, life experience – to come along. As life stretches out its hand, asking us if we wish to join it for the next dance, in that moment we need to ask ourselves whether this invitation is in alignment with what we really want out of life.

Do we accept that invitation (dance) or do we pass? In that moment we need to ask ourselves: 'Will this life experience I'm choosing take me closer to what I truly want to experience? Or will it be yet another dance partner (life experience) that takes me down that same path of unnecessary pain and suffering – the one that always ends with me simply repeating the same bad habits and disconnected decisions?'

'Will this partner throw me around the dance floor and step on my toes? Or worse still, break a few bones so I have to be carted off in an ambulance, confused as to why this has happened, all the while completely oblivious to the fact that I said 'yes' to the same partner the week before and endured the same outcome.' As Einstein famously said: 'Insanity is doing the same thing over and over again and expecting different results.'

So why have I used the word 'invite' in this Question? Well, when we send out an invitation we're requesting someone's presence, but not expecting it as such – it's more that we'd love them to join us. Invitations are open – we don't stop celebrating the event just because the person we invited didn't show up. So in the same way, when we're putting together the things we really want to experience, create and invite into our life, we need to be open to the idea that some will show up and others won't, depending on how aligned they are to where we're at in life and what we truly want.

When we become too obsessed with the outcome of our invitation – or go after something with needy, 'I want' energy – it can actually push whatever it is we want to experience further away. (Trust me, I know!) So, send out the invitation, continue with your life and stay open; pay attention, trust, and surrender to whatever unfolds. It's about connecting to every moment; as everything we need in order to grow is already *in the moment*.

Everything we want is already here

I've learned that when I'm fully connected, everything I need and want is already there – I just need to open my unseen eye and my heart – to a different way of seeing and being.

So many of us stand on the edge of the ocean of our heart's desire, and rather than ask for what we want, we close our eyes and almost 'lucky dip' for it, holding our breath as we wait to see what comes out. Then we'll look over at someone else's life and feel envious of the big, fat, juicy dreams they are getting to experience – moaning because what we have is not what we wanted.

Here in the West, our so-called civilized, advanced, progressive way of living has stripped us of our inherent power. And when I say 'power' I'm not talking about man-made power – the kind that governments and people 'in charge' have. I mean the one that lies within all of us. The power that we find in the stillness, the space, the quiet within that allows us to taste a tiny morsel of who we really are and what we're truly capable of – all of us, from the person living rough on the streets to the Donald Trumps and Oprah Winfreys of this world.

Some call this power the Universe, others call it God, the life force, source. The name is irrelevant, though – what matters is knowing it exists, because it's when we're connected to that space that we *really* know and get that everything we want is already here. It's only in that connected space that we can experience the incredible power of real manifestation!

Real manifestation and self-worth come as one

I've learned that what we manifest or are able to invite into our lives is directly linked to our level of self-worth.

Unless we truly know our worth, and are able to allow things into our lives – to receive them in a way we believe we deserve – it is most likely we'll end up sabotaging whatever it is we've asked for. On many occasions I've put in an order to the Universe, sent off my invitation for what I thought I wanted, and as soon as it arrived I rejected it, or messed about with it so much that I lost it.

And here's why: everything is made of energy – all of us, everything. I am the energy of my beliefs, and my deepest core beliefs have the strongest frequency. So I'm aware that although everything is only a thought away, if I don't believe I *deserve* what I want to attract, then I won't attract it.

This was a big realization for me, especially around my relationships. As I've explained, a great deal of my self-worth and self-love has been linked to my body, and if I look back on the men I've attracted, they have all, on some level, been exactly what I believed I deserved at the time. Every one of them was directly linked to where I was at with my self-worth and self-love. It's ironic then, that as my self-worth improved, so did the men I attracted into my life. But that doesn't mean I still don't push them away or ask myself why they want to be with me.

The last person I fell in love with openly let me know that he loved me but was not physically attracted to me. And while this was painful for me, it was also exactly what I've been saying to myself continuously: I love your personality, Mary, but I'm not physically attracted to you.

Now, as I slowly start to love myself more, I'm learning to love my invitations: to make full-on, passionate love to every opportunity to grow that they bring my way. Even if I'm tempted to run in the opposite direction of an invitation, or to sabotage it, I will take a breath, open up fully, and grab it with both hands. I will feel the fear anyway, love the fear anyway, and give that invitation such a great time that even if it decides to leave the following morning, we'll never forget the amazing journey we had together!

WILD AWAKENING WISDOM

- True manifestation is knowing who we are, connecting to what we really want, and discovering that everything we desire is already available to us.

- Life is not all one way – everything flows. You give, you receive. It's important we remember this when we send out our invitations.

- Before you start writing out a list of everything you think you want to invite into your life, ask yourself *why* you want it. What do you think it will bring or give you?

- I've learned that what we invite into our lives, or are able to manifest, is directly linked to our self-worth and ultimately, self-love: the more we love ourselves the more we'll be able to attract the things that mirror that!

Chapter 6
Wild Women Do

*'The very basic core of a man's living spirit is his
passion for adventure. The joy of life comes from our
encounters with new experiences, and hence there
is no greater joy than to have an endlessly changing
horizon – for each day to have a new and different sun.'*
ALEXANDER SUPERTRAMP – INTO THE WILD

Early in 2015, I was having one of my regular Skype calls with
Mandena, when she suddenly asked me: 'Mary, why don't you
take yourself seriously?' She was frustrated with me – and trust
me, Mandena frustrated is not good: it's like God's finger pointing
at you through the clouds. And while I understood what she was
saying, I didn't really 'get' it.

We'd been talking about my commission from Hay House to write
this book, and about my plan for doing so. From the outset, I'd
known that the timeframe was tight. I had just over three months
to get the first draft written, as well as finalize the contract and
meet some pre-launch marketing deadlines. Alongside this, I was
still working full-time at Alternatives, sorting out my son's needs,
running a home, doing some advisory work and meeting the odd
coaching client. Needless to say, things were pretty crazy.

In fact, the whole period was very intense, from start to finish –
but in one way, that was why I'd agreed to write the book in the

first place. I knew the timing was perfect; I knew I could do 'crazy' well, as in truth, my whole life to date had been crazy, and this was just one more crazy on top of an already high pile of it! I also knew that I loved writing, and let's face it, I'd been living this story for, well, all of my life, so I figured a large part of the book would write itself.

However, as the weeks passed, things at work became quite insane and I had to abandon my original writing plan. Then, with just six weeks to go until my first draft deadline, I figured I needed to test my theory that I could write the book in a month – just in case I was being overly optimistic about my chances (which, ahem, isn't something I'm prone to doing!) When I told other authors about my 'write a book in a month' plan, their jaws dropped in horror!

Mandena had been doubtful about my plans to write the book from the outset. She is well aware that I'm not someone who lives in the 'ordinary' lane of life, but she also knew that this book deal was very important to me, and she felt that, even by my standards, I was pushing things.

By the middle of March I was still sorting bits out at work, and not getting down to much writing, and that's when Mandena posed her question: 'Mary, why don't you take yourself seriously?'

'What do you mean?' I asked.

'Do you want to write this book?'

'I think so,' I replied. 'Yes – yes, of course I do.'

'Then why are you messing around with it; why aren't you taking this seriously? You've known the deadline since the beginning of the year, and even though you now have such a narrow window, you're still messing around, creating the most ridiculous distractions!'

I admitted that I hadn't written half as much as I should have by this point, but a part of me remained optimistic. Calculating the timings, I thought it was still just about possible to meet the deadline. 'I've worked out that if I just wake up at x time, and then do y and z, everything will be fine,' I told Mandena confidently.

She was baffled: how could I think this was a sane plan? 'Mary, that's simply not possible,' she said. 'If I calculate how long it takes to physically type the text, and then proofread, edit and re-type it, I just don't see how you're going to be able to do it!' And then she said something that really freaked me out; it still sends a shiver down my spine when I remember how panicked I felt at the time: 'What would you do if they called you up and cancelled the contract?'

'They wouldn't do that!' I cried, horrified. 'Why would they do that?'

'What would you do – seriously, what would you do?' she went on, before adding: 'In fact, a part of me almost wishes they would!'

'Mandena: don't say that!' I cried again. I was totally freaking out by then. You see, the problem with Mandena is that she's almost always right: she can predict things in ways I haven't seen before, tuning in to her body and almost *feeling* the path your life is going to take. *This is a powerful woman,* I thought. *A woman who has direct access to source! What if she puts in a request for my life path to change?* I wondered whether she could actually do that!

But my mind started to question itself in response to her questions. I thought, *Is this what I want? Yes, I'm certain I want to write a book!* But was I really? Now she had me confused. I'd known for a long time that I wanted to write a book, to share my story in the hope it might inspire or help others, but for some reason I'd sat on the idea for years, and as Mandena said, if I was really that passionate about it, why hadn't I written one already?

Now feeling frustrated and worried, I fell asleep that night with two thoughts whirling around my mind and body: how was I going to pay back my book advance if Mandena put in an order to God/the Universe to cancel the contract!? And why was I so disconnected from the book-writing process? The following morning, with

Mandena's questions weighing heavily on my mind, I left my laptop and went for a walk. I was halfway round my usual park circuit when I started to get it.

Initially, I'd believed I wasn't ready to write my book. I found myself thinking that there are already so many self-help books on the market, what do I have to say that's any different, or even remotely new? Plus, the speakers at the many workshops and courses I've attended were always saying that *we are not our story*, which I got, but it still confused me, as it was always *their* story that had inspired and engaged me in the first place.

At some point I recognized that a big part of me was scared. I was worried that the book would be rubbish; that some members of my family would end up hating me; that Mr Ex would end up feeling demonized by my revelations, and that they would ruin his current relationship; I was worried that people might look at me differently, even be disgusted that I'm not the person they thought I was.

My mind then started to go into free fall. What if my friends think I'm a hippie freak and no longer connect with me? What if my family believe I'm mocking them about their religion and God? What if, what if, what if… And then, out of nowhere, this shifted to: what if the book *does* make a difference to people's lives? What if it turns out I *can* write, and it does have the desired impact? What if, what if, what if…

I told myself: *Mary, this is everything you could have wished for. A book deal handed to you on a plate. Why aren't you grabbing it with both hands?* Why wasn't I, indeed? And then I realized that I hadn't really set a clear intention around what this book was about – I hadn't asked myself *why* I wanted to write it, what message I wanted to put out there, what really mattered to me.

So often over the course of my life I've tried to dumb myself down, always feeling I was too much, too loud, too big, too naughty, too opinionated. So as I was writing the book, I kept censoring myself – saying don't overshare, don't swear too much, don't be too honest or raw, don't use the words God or Universe too much, don't sound too 'out there', and so on and so on. And in the process, I was moving further and further away from who I truly am.

While I was working out what I *really* wanted this book to be about, I suddenly remembered something Mr Italy had once told me: 'Mary, you are not *too* much, you are *so* much!' (A comment that still moves me to this day.) I realized that if I was going to write this book, I had to do it from the only place I knew how – from the real and honest space within me. I had genuinely learned some powerful stuff as a result of my life experiences, and asking myself some real questions, so the answer was simple: Mary, just share your experiences, and share your questions. Just be real and just be you.

So I deleted all the text I'd written to date and started again. Just as I began to get lost in my own journey, I received a WhatsApp message from Mandena: 'Oh dear! I 'feel' this book is now you. I'm so excited and happy for you!'

This woman… I thought. But I smiled, for truth be told, I was excited and happy for me too!

QUESTION 6:
What is my intention, and why?

> *For most of us the problem isn't that we aim too high and*
> *fail. It's just the opposite – we aim too low and succeed.'*
> KEN ROBINSON – *THE ELEMENT*

So why this question? Well, actually, it was something I'd been asking myself for many years, in a way – long before the bridge incident – although it was phrased very differently: 'What do I want to do?' But a few years back, a very powerful realization made me change the Question to something far more meaningful and effective!

At the time I'd been growing tired of life coaching, and was starting to connect to my spirituality and faith again. Despite all the knowledge I'd acquired during my earlier exposure to the world of personal development, I could see that I hadn't really put any of what I'd learned into action. I'd attended lots of so-called 'life-changing' events, but within a few days, I'd discarded everything I'd heard and continued to repeat the same old actions, over and over again! I saw that this was happening for a lot of my friends, too.

And then one day it all fell into place. I realized that I hadn't been questioning the 'why' behind the doing. I'd often find that when I did start 'doing' things, they would become messy, and/or I would become bored very quickly. I observed that this was because I wasn't that connected to the thing I was doing in the first place.

So, instead of focusing on what I was doing, I started to put as much energy into asking myself why I was doing it. I realized that action without meaning is pointless – so I started to ask myself the all-important Question 6: 'What is my intention, and why?' My definition of intention being 'action with meaning and purpose aligned to what you really, really want!'

When I answer this Question, I keep it simple by just focusing on the day ahead, so I ask: 'What is my intention for the day, and why?' Many of us have big goals, and that's great, but if we don't focus on the present moment, it's pointless. And while I have a book of dreams, and things I'd like to create in my life, I believe nothing happens outside of this moment and that no goal is fixed.

In fact, in some ways, a part of me rebels against all the old-school goal-setting: 5-year goals, 10-year goals; I mean come on, most of us can't work out what we want right now, let alone in five years' time. I'm not entirely pooh-poohing the idea of goal-setting, I just think there are pros and cons when it comes to confining ourselves to a linear timeframe. I've found that time is only useful in *some* goal-setting situations, such as meeting a publisher's deadline!

Anyway, the 'why' part of Question 6 is a recent addition, and an important one. Before I go about doing anything, I really try to discover why I want to do it: I ask myself, 'Why do you want to put energy into this?' or 'What do you really think this will give you?' So here are a couple of my answers to the Question: *Today I intend to have one green meal – so I improve my health steadily, instead of constantly being tempted by radical nutritional programmes. Today I intend to spend half an hour sorting out my diary for the week ahead, so I don't forget all the appointments I've agreed to and end up missing one.* (You don't need to use 'Today... each time – sometimes I just start with 'I intend'.)

Below are some of the powerful lessons and insights I've discovered or experienced on a deeper level since I started asking myself this question. If you have any Wild Awakenings – or 'aha' moments – while you read them, make a note of them, and when you start to work through the 9 Questions yourself, which I'll show you how to do in Part III, you can explore what came up for you.

And once again, remember that what follows is based simply on my personal experiences and on my *present* level of awareness, which is continuously deepening, expanding and growing. If you decide you want to challenge, skip, or stay open to anything that doesn't work for you, then feel free: it's your choice.

I need to be real and honest about where I'm at

> *I've learned that before I set an intention it's important that I get real around where I'm at, time-wise, and let go of waiting for the 'perfect moment' or the 'right time'.*

I'm slowly starting to become a little more realistic around what I can and can't achieve within certain timeframes (a lesson learned while writing this book!) I'm a naturally positive, confident and over-ambitious person, but recent events have taught me that setting unrealistic, overly excited, 'emotion-based goals' to get everything done at once can actually suck the joy and fun out of what I'm doing. I thought to myself: *What's the point of doing everything at once if I'm not giving myself enough space to enjoy the rewards of what I'm doing?!*

So, getting more real and honest around where I'm at has meant that, instead of waiting to organize and tidy the spare room when I have a whole weekend free, I'm now spending 30 minutes to an hour a day on it. Rome wasn't built in a day! I've also realized that the quest for perfection, for things to be 'just so', is sometimes a carefully disguised form of procrastination: a well-hidden fear around what it is that needs to be done, or a failure to admit that we actually don't want to do whatever it is we've committed to doing. It's usually the latter for me!

Sometimes we have to make ourselves visible and stand up for what we believe in, or what has meaning for us. Sometimes waiting for the 'right time' to leave that job, start that project, make that call or launch that blog – even write that book – can be a form of avoidance. It's as if we're scared of entering that vulnerable place that exposes us to potential criticisms or knock backs. So it's no wonder that some of us skirt around the edges our entire lives, for fear of not getting things right, failing, having to start again – or worse still, nothing happening.

The act of 'doing' requires us to get off our backsides, to stand for something, invest in ourselves, believe we are worth it. And maybe, instead of being a mindless sheep following the herd of other (often lost) souls, we can navigate our own path – one that's true to who we are and how we want to express ourselves, and that can be a scary place for some of us.

But at some point we need to just get on with it. Otherwise there's a grave danger that we'll simply become spectators to our own potential and possibilities, growing more stagnant and rigid every day until we can no longer move – and that, sadly, is called death! Not pleasant, I know. Even meditation requires us to do something before we let go and do nothing.

I need to stay open to revisiting my plans continuously

*I've learned that sometimes things don't always
go to plan and I need to stay open to revisiting
and revising my original plan continuously!*

Around nine years ago a girlfriend announced she was getting married and asked me to be one of her bridesmaids. This was great on the one hand, but terrifying on the other, as my body confidence was at a real low. Since the birth of my son, I had doubled in size and I hadn't swum or entered the sea on holidays for close to 11 years (and I LOVE the beach, and swimming in the sea even more).

So when a friend of mine who was massively into running marathons suggested I enter the New York Marathon with him, I saw it as a sign. I could lose weight for the wedding (disastrous dress fitting: I was the only bridesmaid who couldn't fit into her dress!); raise money for Cancer Research (a charity that was very close to my heart as I'd lost my foster father, biological father and mother-in-law to the disease); finally visit New York (somewhere I had always wanted to go); and last but not least, tick off 'run a full marathon' on the bucket list!

It was perfect! New York Marathon, here I come, I thought. But did I tell you I was great at setting intentions, but not so great at the planning bit around them? Well, here's a breakdown of what an unplanned intention looks like – Mary style!

Mary's unplanned New York Marathon

1. Made a list of the fears I had about running a marathon. No. 1 – dying on the course. Action: Googled 'how not to die while running a marathon'.

2. Decided on a fundraising target that wouldn't freak me out, but would still be high enough to keep me engaged. Action: £10,000 felt good; done, figure set!

3. Enlisted help to ensure I hit fundraising target.

4. Ten months before the marathon. Still hadn't done any training. Action: made a plan – hit the gym three days a week, run for three days a week, then rest for one day. Also eat a healthy diet. After five months' training, join a running club and work up to running a half-marathon.

5. Reality of the plan: joined the gym and got a great personal trainer who worked out with me once a week and left me with a programme for the rest of the week. Did everything on it – except the running bit!

6. Three months before the wedding/six months before the marathon. Had barely done any running; had lost 10lbs, but still couldn't run a mile! Panicked – joined a slimming club and did a liquid-only diet, while still working out in the gym – stupid idea, but the weight just dropped off.

7. Six weeks before the wedding/four and a half months until the marathon. Dress fitted (slightly too large, in fact, and had it taken in a size!) Still couldn't run a mile, so bought a book called *How to Train for a Marathon in 4 months*!

8. Day of the wedding. Discovered super-slimming underwear that sucks in your tummy to a smaller dress size. Was in love with my new control knickers until they decided to roll down slowly while I was walking up the aisle (true story) – luckily, long dress meant no one noticed them bunched up around my ankles.

9. Marathon three and a half months away. Injured my knee and twisted something in my groin (how, I've no idea). Started physiotherapy and was advised to pull out of marathon: was tempted, but had already raised nearly all the money! Still reading *How to Train for a Marathon in 4 months* – time to come up with Plan C!

10. Marathon two and a half months away. Stopped slimming group, as trainer was horrified when she found out why I was losing so much weight. Still couldn't run a mile!

11. Two months to go. Decided to see how far I could run. Went to Hyde Park, ran for 10 seconds, stopped for 10 seconds. Completed a mile in 14–15 minutes; calculated that if I got that down to 10 minutes, by running for one minute then walking for one minute, multiplied that by 26 then added on 30 minutes for pee stops and stuff, I could complete the marathon in 7 hours. Happy with Plan C!

12. Six weeks to go, and still dodging the trainer. Went to Hyde Park for three or four mornings a week. Ready to join a running club – but still couldn't run a mile!

13. Thirty days to the marathon – joined Serpentine running club in London.

14. Twenty-nine days to marathon – quit the running club.

15. Two weeks to go. Took up power walking and decided that what will be will be.

16. Day of the marathon. Still couldn't run a mile! Back to plan A: just stay alive and hope for the best. Completed marathon in just under 7 hours. VERY HAPPY to be alive!

17. Day after marathon – couldn't walk, had a blister full of blood. Shopping trip cancelled; didn't get to see New York beyond my hotel foyer.

While it's true that a little more planning (well a lot) might have helped my training, and overthinking and over-planning can sometimes kill the passion and mystery that comes from just 'doing', this story beautifully illustrates three things: a) I clearly hate running; b) sometimes you just need to bite the bullet and keep going, even if things aren't going quite to plan; c) sometimes ignorance and simply being in the moment of 'doing' is absolute bliss.

Procrastination = being out of alignment with what we're doing

> I've learned that doing what you love brings meaning to your life and is incredibly energizing. I believe anything that drains us – makes us feel stuck – should be revisited. In fact, if we started changing the word 'procrastination' to 'out of alignment' we might come up with some better, more creative ways of getting things done!

Procrastination is such a big thing. I always used to joke to my friends that you rarely see anyone procrastinating when it comes to having sex! So I thought, what if procrastination simply means we're out of alignment with what we're doing, the way we're doing it or why we are doing what we are doing?

Have you ever had one of those moments when you just hit a wall, or seem to have a block around what you are doing? You know you have the ability to do it, but for some reason it takes you forever to get started. This is procrastination, or blocked energy. I call it being 'out of alignment'. Nowadays when this happens I ask myself three simple questions: 1) Do I really want to do what I am doing? 2) If yes, why? 3) How can I do what I am doing in a way that will bring me the most joy!?

For example, I procrastinate over *doing* my admin. This *doesn't mean* I don't want to be organized – it just means I am not best suited to doing what it takes to get my paperwork in order; so therefore I now have someone who helps me. I also procrastinated over getting this book written in the beginning, not because I didn't want to do it, but because I wasn't aligned with *why* I was doing it and what I wanted the message to be. Once I got clear on that and found a fab spot in the park where I loved to sit and write, I was a happy bunny!

WILD AWAKENING WISDOM

- I've learned that before setting intentions, we really need to take into account what we already know about ourselves. What will make us happy – bring meaning to our lives? It's about setting realistic intentions, managing our expectations and working to our strengths.

- A true intention is an action or a plan with meaning and purpose, aligned to what we really, really want! So before I set my intentions for the day, I ask myself different questions, sometimes as simple as: 'What would make this a powerful day?' or 'What is my true intention behind this action?'

- It's better to take a little action every day, than wait for the 'perfect moment' and blitz the whole thing. Perfectionism is sometimes procrastination in disguise.

- Planning for things is great, and at times absolutely essential, but sometimes over-planning and overthinking can squeeze the fun, joy and passion out of simply 'doing'.

- Procrastination can be a great opportunity to ask ourselves, *Do I really want to be doing what I am doing, and if so, why and how do I want to do it?*

Chapter 7

Don't Give Up

*'You have to leave the city of your comfort and go into
the wilderness of your intuition. What you discover
will be wonderful. What you'll discover is yourself.'*

Alan Alda

I've always had a strong sense of trust in life – looking back, I can
see that it has always provided for me, and that I've bounced from
one great opportunity to the next without really doing much. For
example, I was asked to become a volunteer at Alternatives, and
then to become their workshop coordinator; finally I was asked to
become co-director of the organization.

I got into youth coaching following a conversation with a friend,
and that led me to the Prince of Wales's charity Mosaic, which in
turn opened the door to Future Foundations, and working with
thousands of young people up and down the UK. I'm now part of
one of the largest national Social Action programmes for teenagers!
Hay House invited me to write this book. I wanted to go to Italy, and
to do more group coaching work, and the next thing I knew a friend
had moved to Italy, got a great job working with Tribewanted, and
invited me over to look at running retreats there.

So, trusting in life has always been easy, and it was something I
took for granted – until recently, that is. When I first accepted the

role of co-director of Alternatives, I underestimated the amount of work it would involve. I know a lot of people believed we just sat around all day, listening to meditations and chants, occasionally pulling an 'Angel Card' and calling someone we liked the 'feel' of to come and give a talk. But, as with any organization or business, as much as we loved what we did, it was incredibly hard work.

As well as hosting up to four events a week, and managing an ongoing programme, the team had to juggle a large volume of calls, enquiries, emails and requests from speakers around the world. We had to address the needs of the venues, the speakers, the volunteers and our community, all the while spreading the news about what we were up to, and find engaging ways of sharing our message. Altogether it was full-on, and as the team was small, part-time, and had a limited budget and resources, we were having to be continuously creative!

I was very passionate about what we were doing, and what it all stood for, and over time, I started to let the boundaries between my work and my home life slip. I'd often take on tasks or say 'yes' to things I simply didn't have the capacity, or the skillset, to do – and sometimes this involved working round the clock and getting home late into the evening.

As my workload increased, my downtime became swallowed up by my job, and I slowly started to drown, hitting a wall of exhaustion several times. In truth, I'm surprised I was surprised that this happened, as this way of working has been an ongoing pattern throughout my life. Lack of boundaries!

I felt guilty that I wasn't there enough for my then 17-year-old son (even though he said he loved the freedom it gave him!) I was also struggling to keep on top of my personal paperwork, hardly saw any of my friends – I constantly bumped our arrangements and appointments – and my family scarcely got a look in. I couldn't work it out: how could someone who 'knew' so much have allowed things to spin out of control?

My life was becoming a mess because I was becoming a mess. And then that was when it happened – out of nowhere. The holding on for dear life and mask of control slipped and I had a thought I'd not had for years: *Mary, just end it – no one will care and this unbearable pain will be all over in seconds.* I hadn't had a suicidal thought like that in many, many years – in fact, not since the bridge – and I'd promised myself I would never go back there again. That was the whole point of my Daily Prep: to stay connected!

Luckily, the thought lasted just a couple of minutes, and despite my disappointment at allowing myself to get to that place, I could see how the work I'd done on myself had at least allowed me to recognize and catch it before it quickly descended into an action. I was more alarmed, though, by how good that thought had felt – and I mean *really* good: as if every cell in my body could breathe out. It was an amazing sense of bliss – as if I'd injected a drug that would completely take away all the pain.

I knew I urgently needed time out, and so I was relieved that I had a trusted friend coming over to visit. Too numb to feel guilty about walking away from critical deadlines, I left the office. All I knew was, if I was going to survive this, I needed to put myself first. My friend and I disappeared for three days – down to the stunning Jurassic coast in Dorset, in the southwest of England.

Hidden away in a little barn/cottage with no internet and no phone, I immersed myself in nature, remembering what it felt like simply to be. Those few days felt like an eternity; we spent our time walking down to the beach, discovering the coastline, crashing out on the sofa, talking, cooking and doing nothing. All of this made me appreciate the power of being around nature, and the connection to another human being – which, ultimately, opens up the connection to yourself. By the end of our time there, I was reconnecting – I was starting to feel like myself again! I had found me.

In many ways that trip saved my life, and on reflection I noticed how I'd really let my practice slide. I'd stopped walking in nature, stopped doing my 9 Questions, stopped meditating; I hadn't even been in my garden. In fact, I had dropped my entire Daily Prep, and just a year after my miraculous awakening in Italy, I was almost back to square one! And that's when I knew that I needed to return to my Daily Prep.

I thought to myself, *If I can't spare just nine minutes a day to answer my Questions, then something is seriously wrong with my life.* (Obviously, the other parts of my Daily Prep were important too, but I knew it always started with the 9 Questions.) If I was going to stay connected to me – if I was to be my own guiding compass, my trust, my inner voice – I needed to make time.

QUESTION 7:
I trust

> *'Surrender is not giving up, far from it. Surrender takes an enormous amount of courage. Often we are only capable of doing so when the pain of trying to control the outcome becomes too much to bear.'*
>
> BRONNIE WARE – *THE TOP FIVE REGRETS OF THE DYING*

So Question 7 is all about trust! I love this question, even though it only recently appeared on the list. As I've explained above, trust and self-belief are things I've realized I have a lot of in my life – not because I've identified this in myself, but more because people have seen it in me and told me so.

But after experiencing a couple of incidents in my life where I really lost that connection with my sense of knowing and trust – like the one I've described above – I realized how important it is for me to always stay connected to myself. In a nutshell, trust is all about total connection to self – trust is that inner voice, that guiding compass, the GPS of the soul I talked about earlier that continuously redirects us back to our 'self'.

For me, real trust is about being able to totally surrender to 'what is': being able to let go – into the unknown, the uncertain. It's about releasing control and totally trusting that knowing space and voice within us, our intuition. The bottom line is, when you are completely trusting, you are totally connected – manifesting and creating the life you really want.

Now I'm sure you've noticed that the words 'I trust' don't actually form a question, and there's a good reason for this. If I'd phrased this Question like the others on my list, creating something like, 'Where is my trust?' 'What do I trust?' 'Who do I trust?', my response to it would not have connected with the pure meaning of the words.

So in order to stay true to the words, when I answer Question 7 I start by writing 'I trust' and then I just jot down whatever comes into my mind in order to complete the phrase. For example, when I did this recently, this is what came out: *I trust that I will be able to deal with all the changes that are happening in my life. I trust that everyone who is mentioned in this book is happy with what I've shared, and feels that I've represented them and our relationship/ exchange with integrity. I trust in life and where this new journey is taking me.*

So, as you can see, there's no right or wrong way to respond to this 'Question'; when you come to answer it yourself, just write the words 'I trust' and the rest of the phrase will follow naturally. It's really important that you don't force this one – part of the process is about trusting whatever comes out for you.

So, below are some of the insights that have come out of my completing the phrase 'I trust...' As before, these are based simply on my personal experiences and on my *present* level of awareness, which is continuously deepening, expanding and growing. So please go with what works for you, and if you want to challenge, skip, or stay open to anything that doesn't, then feel free: it's your choice.

I need to slow down to connect to trust

*I've learned that the signs are always there and that
life always has our best interests at heart – sometimes
we simply need to slow down and listen more.*

I've learned that life is always working with our best interests at heart, even in the moments when it feels as if things aren't turning out the way we'd planned, or seem particularly challenging. I've noticed when things start to feel this way it doesn't mean there's something wrong with our life, or that what life had planned for us is failing. Instead, it usually means our 'soul needs us to grow' and has therefore invited new experiences into our life.

As long as we stay tuned in, slow down and keep our eyes open we'll spot the subtle messages that are trying to guide us. If we feel we're off track it's probably because we ignored that quiet whisper within that we call our intuition; or perhaps we're too scared to see the truth of what's unfolding in front of us.

Whatever the reason, if we look back on our lives really closely and are truly honest with ourselves we'll soon see that the signs were always there. They may have been in the shape of a new job opportunity, a so-called chance meeting with someone, or life blatantly pointing out: 'happy, fulfilled, abundant and peaceful life, thatta way'.

Trust can produce miracles

*I've learned that I must never take my trust for granted, and
that having faith and trusting in myself always pays off.*

Not long after the end of my 18-year relationship I had to find a new home for myself and my son within a period of just eight days. We'd been living in a four-bed flat in a mansion block, but I could no longer afford the rent, so I decided we needed to downsize to a two-bed flat very quickly.

There was a great deal to be done and very little time to do it. I needed to work out which area of London I could afford to live in; organize the home office – all the furniture and paperwork I'd stored in the basement, which was a lot; sort and pack up clothes and belongings, and get rid of things we couldn't take with us.

On top of that I had to secure more work – in order to pay for our new home – and find a new school for my son for the following term. So, with all that facing me, I headed off to work one Saturday (I was doing weekends at Alternatives as their workshop coordinator). At the end of the day, as I stood outside the office, the then director, Steve, came over for a chat about my forthcoming move.

'Mary, for someone who has just over a week to get everything done, you seem very relaxed,' he remarked.

I laughed and said, 'I'm trusting that I'll get it sorted in time.'

'Do you even know which area you want to live in?' he asked.

'No, not yet,' I replied. 'I'll look tonight or tomorrow.'

Laughing, as if to say, I don't know how you do it, Steve turned to me and said, 'I hope that one of your Questions is about trust,' and with that he rode off on his bike. As I made my way home I thought, *Hmm, trust: why would I add that to my Questions?* And it was at that point that I realized that trust is the one thing in my life I've always had an incredible amount of, so I didn't feel I needed to work on it.

Then, a few days later, and running out of time on the move, I decided to go to bed and dream of my ideal flat. The next morning I decided I was going to be really specific and ask for *exactly* what I wanted and had dreamed of. Thinking I'd have some fun before getting down to a serious search, I keyed in my requirements: 'garden flat, newly refurbished, near a park, laundry room, storage, a period property that feels safe, two bedrooms, nice bathroom…'

Four potential properties came up – two had already been let, one was about to be... but then, there it was: my ideal flat! It was beautifully refurbished, with *everything* I'd described – right down to the colour of the flooring. It even had two outside spaces instead of one, and was in a prime location in London. It was just beyond my budget, but something inside told me I would be able to work this out.

As I went about securing this flat, everything that could go wrong did, but still I just knew it would become my next home. I could see myself and my son there – it felt right in the core of my body. So I kept going, and two days before I was due to move I had a lovely call from the agent: I had the all-clear. I nearly cried – yet again, that 'knowing' feeling had paid off... phew! The following morning I added 'I trust' to my then seven Questions: not because at the time I needed more trust, but because I didn't want to take it for granted.

Trust never goes away

I've learned that trust and connection to self are one and the same.

Sometimes our spiritual path requires us to venture into the unknown – to go to terrifying places where the only way out is to truly surrender – and that's when our trust is tested. But we need to trust that, no matter what – and I mean no matter what – all is well. Not all *will* be well, but all *is and will always be well.*

For most of us, this is very difficult – especially since the world can seem very scary when it feels as if trust has completely disappeared. As I've said, I've always relied very heavily on trust – in fact, at times it's been the one thing that's got me through some very dark periods in my life. I've experienced first-hand that when you're in the heart of the pain, and your world seems so dark, it can be very hard to hang on to that self-belief and 'knowing' that all will be well.

In fact, there have been times when my thoughts have become so heavy, they have completely blocked or drowned out any sense of knowing – and it felt almost impossible that any light could get through the cracks. But that is when I see my trust in life, and with the support of my friends and family, I've pulled through.

What I've really come to recognize is that my sense of trust and knowing comes as one. It's a constant life force, a divine presence, an incredible energy. Trust doesn't come or go: when someone says, 'I don't know how to trust', or 'I've lost my trust', what they are really saying is: 'I'm lost; my sense of self has gone, and I'm no longer connected.' That can be a very scary place, but take comfort in the knowledge that as soon as you reconnect to yourself, you'll reconnect to your sense of trust.

Trust is letting go of control

I've learned that real trust requires faith. It's about learning to let go of the outcome – to release the need to control, and totally surrender to self.

I'm someone who likes to 'know' things; I like to know where things are headed, what the outcome will be, what others are thinking. Essentially, I like to know that I'm in control of things. But why? It's because on some level I *don't* trust – or more accurately, I can struggle to surrender to something. And there lies the contradiction in my behaviour: on the one hand I'm very trusting, but on the other I'm a bit of a control freak over my own life. (This is why you should be careful of people who profess to know it all: luckily, I'm a mess, so you're fine!)

So I'm striving to surrender to my trust in life, God, the Universe, and ultimately myself: not because I have all the answers, or even need them, but because everything I need in order to grow and get me through this life is always available to me. In fact, it has always shown itself when I really needed it to.

So why does it feel so scary sometimes, to surrender to our trust in life? I guess in one way it's because we are trusting the 'unseen'.

It's like that feeling we get when we fall backwards into someone's arms – a part of us is not sure they'll catch us, so we keep looking over our shoulder to make sure they're ready: standing in the right position so we can see them.

I can see that my need to know the outcome is like that – as if I'm constantly looking over my shoulder to see if life is ready to catch me. However, because *I am life*, in one silly way, what I'm really saying is, *Mary, do you think you can catch and hold yourself? Have you got you?*

I need to trust my body, and my intuition

> *I've learned to trust the feelings I have in my body; my intuition is never wrong.*

I connect to my feelings in so many different ways. I've often been told that I'm highly intuitive, and recently, a lot of people have also said I'm a clairsentient – someone who feels things in their physical body. What I have noticed is that I'm driven by what I feel in my body in certain situations, and then I'm able to put that into pictures or words, and find my way through a situation. This is something we all do: perhaps not always consciously. If you've ever met someone or been in a situation where you've thought, *Hmm, I have a really bad vibe about this*, that's what I'm describing.

I know a lot of people who've learned to really tune in to this intuition in a powerful way (I am still a kid in a candy store with mine). I have to say that Mandena's intuitive gifts are incredible: inside, I'm always joking that I need to be pretty clear on what I'm saying or feeling when I speak to her, as she can pick it up in a heartbeat. And not that I need to, or do, but lying to her would be an utter waste of time!

I usually trust my intuition above anything else and have learned that ignoring it is dangerous: recently, something happened to me that reinforced this message. I've been taking heed of Mandena's direct feedback on a certain habit I've acquired. I used to have a tendency to throw my debit card into my handbag after using it, but recently I've started putting it back into my wallet instead. However, the other day, while I was out shopping with a friend, I had to pay for something very quickly, and as the cashier handed back my debit card, I hurriedly shoved it inside my handbag.

A voice inside me said: *Mary, just slow down: put it straight back in your wallet and be done with it, so you know where it is for next time.* Then, just as quickly as that intuitive voice spoke, my mind stepped in and said, *Don't worry, forget it: we'll have plenty of time to do it in the car.* (Remember, intuition speaks before the mind, and is always quieter; however, if you ignore it, it will leave you to it.) Anyway, my friend and I returned to the car and off we went.

The following day, I'd been working hard and was starving, so I thought I'd go for a bite to eat. An hour later, after ordering my food, I went to pull out my wallet to pay for it. But the debit card wasn't there! OMG, I thought; what the… Then I remembered the internal conversation I'd had with myself the previous day. I smiled and my inner voice said: *I did warn you.*

Luckily, in that particular café, you have to pay for the food before it's served, so I cancelled my original order and, with only a handful of change in my pocket, I left with a bag of potato wedges. As I walked home, my mind said: *Could have been worse.* To which my stomach replied: *Oh do shut up.*

I can't trust my thoughts!

I'm learning to be very careful of my thoughts – especially when they start stirring up my emotions and insecurities!

I've learned not to trust my thoughts. This is a realization that really hit home after a couple of recent events. One day I was 'feeling' so anxious about something it was overwhelming. When I asked myself where this so-called feeling was emanating from, I realized it was coming from my thoughts.

It was a fear – an unreal one – that had been created by my thoughts, and it was so powerful I could feel it in my body. When I went underneath the feeling I could see how the fear had been stirred up by my thinking that if I didn't get something completed, I would lose the opportunity. It was the fear of loss.

After a conversation with Mandena in which she asked me if I really knew the difference between my emotions and my feelings, I started to pay more attention to the two. A relationship had recently come to an end and I was feeling so many different emotions – from hurt to intense anger – so I decided to take a step back and really connect with her question, and it was then that I noticed something really powerful around my emotions. I realized that, instead of stepping back from my emotions about this in the way I knew I should – i.e. sitting with them – I was going crazy with them. And the result was more of my usual Jekyll and Hyde behaviour: the disaster Mr Italy always talks about.

I started to observe that this 'attachment' to things and people, this fear of loss, was really at the heart of my pain and suffering. As soon as I calmed my thoughts around this, my emotions calmed down too, and I realized the problem was not that I was 'too' emotional but that I was creating these emotional responses through my thoughts and attachments.

Mary, you really need to watch your thoughts, I thought. This attachment to certain outcomes – to the way things *should* play out in life – went a lot deeper than I'd realized. The more I see that my emotions are a result of a thought that involves a belief or an attachment to an outcome – an ideal or a way of being that's being threatened – the more I realize the sheer number of ways I'm being triggered in this way. And how I'm constantly responding to so many of those triggers without even realizing it! Jeez, as if I didn't already have enough on the 'sort out your life, Mary' list!

We need to trust ourselves over others

*I've learned that it's crazy to rely on and put **all** our trust in others. We need to take responsibility for where our life is headed. If we don't know what we want for ourselves, how on earth can we expect someone else to really know what's best for us?*

We all know how painful it feels when a close friend hurts us. We never forget it, which is why people say that once someone's trust has been broken it is very hard to fix it. We see this in our relationships all the time – we go into them with unspoken, unconscious, unrealistic expectations – placed on ourselves and the 'other' person. In fact, I often think the real reason behind a divorce is 'You are not what I expected; this relationship is not what I expected; I thought you would change, or that over time I would be able to change you, rather than truly accept you (real love).'

Basically, we live off the potential of something rather than the reality. And if we are 'in love', well, let's face it, most of us are screwed. That pink potion of loved-up whatever will make us create, believe and live out any reality we choose, so we'd better hope that all parties involved are in love and stay in love, because if one wakes up from the drug, Lord almighty, what a difference *that* day will make!

I *know* – cheerless and bitter old me: sorry. Anyway, fundamentally, I believe it's dangerous to put our trust in others. We are only human, and we'll mess up or not do as we are told. We don't always mean to do this, but often we can't help it.

Much of the time we're all still figuring out our own stuff, and even with the best awareness and intentions in the world, most of us don't know what we want and wouldn't have a clue what *real* looked like if it undressed slowly in front of us in the form of our hottest fantasy! And even when we think we do, there's still something else beneath that, driving it, so we're constantly changing our minds. This is a subject that Adyashanti explores beautifully in his book *Fall from Grace.*

I'm not saying that I don't have some great, trusted friends, but the long and the short of it is: trust yourself above all others. If you trust yourself, follow *your* heart, figure out what *you* really want and live your life for *you*, it won't matter what 'others' are or aren't doing.

WILD AWAKENING WISDOM

- I've learned that as long as I find ways to stay connected to myself, I will never lose my sense of trust – for connection and trust are one and the same thing.

- I've learned never to take my trust for granted, and that having faith in myself, life, always pays off.

- Trust is never about another person – it's about trusting yourself. If you can completely trust yourself, you need never worry about trusting others. In fact, trust is acting as if the other person doesn't exist.

- I've learned that putting our trust in others is merely putting an expectation on them, and expectations of any kind eventually end up in some form of disappointment – simply because we are human.

- I've learned that as long as I trust myself there is no need for me to try and control and manage others or outcomes. Trust is letting go of control and allowing total surrender to self.

- I've learned that the signs pointing us in the right direction are always there – we just need to slow down and trust that inner whisper.

Chapter 8

Beneath Your Beautiful

'Close your eyes, fall in love, stay there.'
RUMI

As a Hay House author, I share the next story with a big smile on my face. A few years back I attended a two-day workshop by Louise Hay and Cheryl Richardson. Thanks to my spirit junkie friends, who had camped outside the venue at ridiculous o'clock, we were sat right in the front row, up close and personal with two of Hay House's queens.

I had no idea what the first day had in store for us but, having seen Louise Hay once before, and being a big fan of Louise and Cheryl's no-nonsense coaching style, I was excited to see them both in action. From the outset, Louise was real, honest and gritty – all the things I love in a teacher. She got straight to the point: explaining the lessons without any unnecessary fluff. So to say I was enjoying the workshop would be an understatement. Well, that is until Louise uttered the dreaded words – the ones I'd hoped to escape:

'Now I want everyone to reach into his or her bag and pull out the mirror.' Arrghhh – I hated this sort of thing. Mirror work: what a waste of time that was, lying to my reflection in a mirror. If I'd been sitting further back, and was not there as a representative of Alternatives, I'd have made my excuses and left. As I reluctantly reached for my bag and pulled out the mirror I'd been handed on the way in, I noticed the following words in fluorescent pink: 'Life loves you'.

Oh my gosh, I thought, can this get any worse!? (At the time, I was unaware that this is one of Louise's best-loved affirmations – remember, I was a latecomer to the world of self-love!)

As I listened to people saying Louise's affirmation, I thought to myself, *Life didn't love me yesterday, when I was stuck in a traffic jam for two hours while taking my son to school; nor did it love me when the police pulled me over for turning the car around in the middle of the road – after my poor son had sat tired and wheezing in the traffic; and it certainly didn't love me when the police didn't stop any of the three taxi drivers who did exactly the same manoeuvre as I'd done, at the same time. No, they only stopped me!*

I faked an enthusiastic smile as the friend sitting next to me excitedly opened her mirror. I was unable to open mine properly – I turned it sideways and spotted that the middle section was broken and that one part of the mirror was cracked. *Typical!* I thought. Finally, I put the half-broken mirror up to my face, looked at my reflection and said, 'Mary, life loves you', all the while joking and laughing with my friend. Nothing happened: there was no self-love, no warm fluffy arms around me. I didn't feel a thing; actually, tell a lie, by this point I felt hungry and needed lunch.

To be continued!

QUESTION 8:
I love

*'All life is a manifestation of the spirit,
the manifestation of love.'*
MORIHEI UESHIBA

This has been one of my 9 Questions for a while now, but over time I have come to connect with it in *two* completely different ways, and it has actually become very powerful. It has taken me a while to get into doing it this way, but now I *love* it! When I answer this Question I look at it from a personal perspective – what I love about myself – and from the perspective of universal love, as I call it – what I love about life itself. For the personal view, I look at parts of my body, my personality; I note that everything about me is absolutely perfect and that *I am life*. Like daily love notes to myself! Here are some examples: *I love my tummy and the way my fat still holds shape – as if it's really trying hard to become muscle! I love my smile. I love the way my eyes light up like a child's when I'm excited!*

And here are some examples from the universal love perspective: *I love the way my life is totally reflected around me, and my son, and that I am connected to everything. I love the way music makes my soul come alive. I love this planet and I love my life.*

But, of course, like 'I trust', the Question 'I love' takes a different form to the other Questions. If I'd used the words 'I love' to create a direct question – 'What/Who do I love?' or 'Where is my love?' – my response would have taken me away from the purity of the words themselves. So in order to stay true to them, when I answer Question 8 I start by writing 'I love' and then I just jot down whatever comes into my mind in order to complete the phrase (see examples above).

Below are some of the really powerful realizations, insights and lessons I've discovered since I started to complete the phrase 'I love'. As you read them, if you have any Wild Awakenings – or 'aha' moments – make a note of them, and when you start to work through the 9 Questions yourself, you can explore what came up for you. Finally, what follows is based simply on my personal experiences and on my *present* level of awareness, which is continuously deepening, expanding and growing. So please go with what works for you, and if you want to challenge, skip, or stay open to anything that doesn't, then feel free: it's your choice.

Love swapping

*I've learned that we use love like a currency, with many of us not really knowing what it means to **be** love.*

Nowadays we use the word 'love' like a currency: I'll give you some love if you give me some in return. And the three simple words 'I love you' have become over-used, deeply misunderstood and chased as if our lives depended on it. But relax, I'm not a cynic or a love grump – I actually love love: how could I not?

But, in fact, *love is what we are.* So many of us have been taught how to seek love, but not how to connect to the love that we are, to *be love* (a concept that sounds crazy in some ways). When I say that we've been taught to love, what I mean is, how many times have we heard someone say, 'Well, that's not very loving,' or 'If you really loved me, you would do or say x, y or z.'? Or they say: 'How can you call that love when you do those things?' When we're young, we hear our parents say things like, 'How much does mummy love you?' and 'Give auntie a kiss and tell her how much you love her.'

So at many different points in our lives we're 'told' how to love, as opposed to being shown how to 'be love'; basically to accept and know who we are. Unconditional love is the kind of love that requires nothing back – it's pure acceptance of the whole. This is something few people, including myself, truly realize. During one of my many conversations with Mr Italy about love, I remember him saying, 'As soon as you put "is" after the word love, you've already moved away from what love truly is.' I immediately got what he meant.

I remember when Mr Ex first told me he loved me. I was so excited to hear it, but I also recall thinking, *How amazing: he loves me! I now need to tell him I love him too, even though I'm terrified by what this means – and I'm not even sure whether I do love him. I definitely know my feelings don't match the way he is looking at me… but if I don't say something in return, that will be mean, awful. And then what? Will he leave me? No longer want me? What if no one else loves me like this again?*

My memories of the love I experienced with Mr Ex always remind me of a video by singer Roger Sanchez, for a song called 'Another Chance'. It starts off with a girl wandering around a city carrying a huge heart, the size of her entire body. Then, over the course of the evening, as people reject her, ignore her and look at her as if she were weird, the heart slowly shrinks, until it's so small the girl can easily hold it in both hands; it's still visible to passers-by, but it's significantly smaller. At this point a man makes a comment about the girl's heart that I'll never forget:

'Is that your heart?' he asks.

'Yeah,' she says.

'It's big,' he says. To which she responds, 'It is small now: it was bigger before.'

'Scary,' he says.

Anyway, the girl goes out with the man and of course her heart starts to get bigger and bigger. You need to watch the end of the video, as its depiction of the way love is so often experienced is really cool. I love this video, as it's spot-on as a representation of my own experiences of love, and some of my friends.

But what it really showed me is that we search for love outside of ourselves. It's as if we're in a market place – looking for places to buy and sell love, and exchanging a bit of our 'heart' for love. Which is why when a relationship ends we feel as if someone has taken a part of us; or when we come to love a person who has entered our life we say that person 'completes' us! But we are not half a person: we are a whole person!

Receiving love, and self-love

I've learned that it's impossible to receive love if we can't connect to the love that we are. I'm learning that the level of love we can receive is equal to the level of love we have for ourselves.

A couple of years after Mr Ex and I had separated I ended up dating a beautiful man – a bundle of love. He was literally everything I had wished for at that moment: a 6 feet 4 inch, dark-haired teddy bear who drowned me in love (I'm noticing I have a thing about height; anyway I shall call him Teddy Bear G). It was as if Louise Hay had conspired with God and sent me the biggest walking mirror of 'life loves you' she could find.

However, although he sent me a bunch of flowers every week, picked me up from work, cooked for me, was endlessly thoughtful, was into the same music as me, was a doer around the house, loved *Dr Who* (I'm a massive fan) and was amazing in bed (something I'd really missed), I just couldn't receive his love: it was as if a part of me had shut down and was rejecting it.

I was always questioning the love: whether I was attracted to him, whether he was really attracted to me – basically, always questioning and going hot and cold. I'd often push him away and almost constantly tested him on why he was with me. I found his love suffocating, and often questioned what was missing; it was as if I didn't value it or feel I deserved it.

Although he told me he had never felt so loved and cared for, I could see my constant questioning was starting to wear him down. Until one day he told me that he'd never felt so lonely in a relationship. Well, that broke my heart, and I knew that I not only needed to end it, I really needed to work on my issues of self-love.

So, I turned back to Louise Hay's mirror work – not yet ready to face the 'real' mirror called life. I decided I was going to take a year off from relationships and dating and embark on learning how to fall in love with myself. This started off really well until, despite all my efforts not to, I went and fell in love! Disaster!

For me, the feeling of 'in love' is not the same as real love

I've learned that being 'in love' is not the same as 'real love'. In love usually carries an expectation, an attachment, a need – and if this doesn't work out it can sometimes leave us experiencing a sense of loss, even rejection.

So, as I mentioned earlier, things between me and Mr Italy eventually became intense. We'd gone from messaging or speaking to each other every now and then, to being in contact very frequently – sometimes every day (we'd talk until the early hours – which was painful for him as he *loves* his sleep!)

Anyway, as I'm sure you've guessed, it was only a matter of time before Miss Disaster ended up falling in love. Bloody pink potion – what a pain in the arse! I hate being in love! And on this occasion it was a rollercoaster ride that went from crazy, messy and emotional, to exhilarating highs, learning and intense connections – and then right back down to total heartache, low self-esteem and feelings of intense rejection.

Anyway, at the end of all the turmoil I was able to stand back and laugh at it all – Mr Italy and I now call this 'my crazy period' – and while we both admitted that we'd experienced this weird, intense, almost soul love/connection for each other, he himself was not taken by the pink potion. However, let me take you back in time to what happened *before* we reached that place of clarity; let me explain how this 'in love' thing all kicked off.

At the outset of our friendship I'd decided on the 'act cool, and talk about things you both enjoy' approach, hoping to just let things unfold naturally. I decided I didn't want to make a big deal out of my feelings, and just hoped they'd pass. Well, that was a waste of time! As you well know by now, staying cool and keeping my emotions in check are still a big work in progress for me!

I'd fire off between four and eight emails a day to him – most of them reading like blog entries about my day and my various emotions and insights – while avoiding telling him I loved him. All this did was start to scare him. Eventually, after a few chats with Mandena (actually, several long conversations), she said: 'Just *tell* him how you feel; I don't get it: why don't you just tell him?'

Was she mad? Why would I do that? Clearly she hadn't heard of the cool approach. Why would I tell someone I knew wasn't in love with me, that I was in love with him? Who does that to themselves? Why invite rejection on a massive scale? Anyway, I said, I didn't need to tell him anything. I wasn't looking for a relationship – I just liked talking to him.

'Mary, remember your lessons – life is simple, say what you want, be honest. You love him and you want to know if he loves you too. Simple, like a child, remember?' So one day I decided to bite the bullet and tell him exactly how I felt. Five or six rehashed emails later, I finally spat the words out. I told him how I felt – that I wanted nothing from him, but had decided I didn't want to play games any more and that it actually felt good just getting it off my chest.

And to be honest, it did feel good. I felt much lighter and as soon as I said it I realized I didn't even need a response from him. It was not about what he did or didn't feel, but more about how I felt: just being true to myself.

Well, you know the saying be careful what you wish for? That's what I got back – nothing; no response to any more of my messages. There it was, my good old friend rejection – straight to the heart! I spent the next few weeks licking my wounds, picking myself up and getting back on the broken buggy of self-love.

At one point, Mandena called me to check in on how the lovesick puppy was doing. And the conversation we had then has changed my life and altered my approach to love completely! It went a little bit like this.

I was midway through an explanation of why I was 'in love' with Mr Italy when she suddenly stopped me and asked what I meant by 'in love'. I gave her a definition, but it must have left her unimpressed, because she asked the question again. Slowing down this time, I thought about it more deeply. And I confessed that I *kind of knew* what I meant by it, but I couldn't put it into words: it's the initial physical reaction you get when you meet someone you really like...

Then she asked me: 'What do you mean when you say you are "in love" with him?' Oh gosh, I thought, my responses are not going down well here. But I was confident I could answer this one: she'd said 'in love *with him*', so I talked about his qualities – how he made me feel, the great conversations we had, the laughter... it was like a shopping list of things he did, and in return how that made me feel.

I think the pain of me going on was too much for Mandena, because she simply said: 'Mary, who is this 'other' person? There is no such thing as an 'other' – this is only about you.' At first I pulled my 'I get it' face, but then I admitted that I didn't get it at all – which I knew she knew. So she continued to ask me a few more questions until I think we both knew that although I did get it intellectually, it would take time for me to actually experience it and *really* get it.

So after the call, I was determined to crack this 'there is no such thing as an "other"' thing. I decided to pretend to myself that I'd got it, and every time I became worked up by the way the object of my affections didn't answer my messages or return my calls, I kept saying to myself: *Mary, there is no such thing as an 'other'; the other person doesn't exist, he is just a mirror – a reflection of what is going on inside of you. This is only about you. What is this teaching you about yourself?*

I did this over and over again, each time feeling some form of lack, a weird kind of rejection, a loneliness, a slight panic and the pain of knowing there was no 'he' waiting there for me, wanting to be with me. So every time I missed him or wanted him to respond to me in a certain way, show me he loved me in *some* way, I kept telling myself, *Mary, there is no such thing as an 'other'; this is only and all about you. What is it telling you about yourself? What is it you want from him that you are not giving to yourself? What does this space represent?*

I just wished I could meet someone who would see me for who I am: not judge me or reject me because of my size; or want me because I could entertain them, look after them, provide for them, inspire them or make them proud of me. I longed for a relationship in which the person would be my friend first and lover second; someone who was my equal, with whom I could talk, have fun, explore the world, and engage in mind-blowing conversations that would keep us up all night. Someone who would excite all my senses…

But then I would return to the painful space of *Mary, this is not about an 'other' person: what he can give you, and this fantasy of a space you believe you can only create with him. There is no 'other' – there is nothing outside of yourself; everything is a mirror pointing back to within you.*

I did this exercise repeatedly, until one day I got it: like a palm slap to my forehead. He hadn't rejected me: I had rejected me. I hadn't seen me; I hadn't thought I was good enough. I'd thought I was too fat, unlovable, not worthy – it was all me. He had nothing to do with it; in fact, in the nicest sense, he didn't factor at all.

> '*Self-knowledge involves relationship. To know oneself is to study one's self in action with another person. Relationship is a process of self-evaluation and self-revelation. Relationship is the mirror in which you discover yourself – to be is to be related.*'
> BRUCE LEE

This was all one huge mirror: an opportunity for me to see myself – to see how much I really did or didn't love myself. It was like Louise Hay's mirror work in full force, and because I did not love me, or see myself as beautiful, the mirror called 'my life' was reflecting that straight back at me. I had got it, but finally I felt what it meant in my body. Finally the pain started to subside and instead I felt a great sense of joy, of freedom, of finally feeling loved and accepted.

Well, the day after this latest epiphany I went straight out and bought myself a beautiful little gilded mirror and, trying to avoid focusing on the absence of make-up and the little lines across my face, I stared into my eyes and said the words, 'Life loves you'. Smiling, I said it again, and then finally I repeated it once more, noticing only my beautiful smile and the shiny little girl reflected back at me through my eyes. 'Mary, life loves you!'

After a few days of doing this, standing half-naked in front of my large bathroom mirror, I leaned over, gave myself a kiss and said, 'You know what, Mary: I LOVE YOU!' It was the most amazing feeling in the world, and one I've been working on, slowly, bit by bit, ever since.

So in conclusion, does this mean that I've 'cracked' love? Hell no, this is a muscle I will forever have to exercise. Does this also mean I now love being 'in love', or can stop myself from falling in love? No, of course not; I love real love and I still despise falling 'in love', and if I could avoid that pink cloud of in-love chemical reaction that gets me higher than Black Sabbath on tour, I would. However, at least I know, as I keep working at this, that I have a choice as to how I approach this space – knowing it is never about the 'other' person and all about how I connect to and love myself!

The journey of self-love never ends

I've learned that whenever we feel we can't live without something or someone, we have moved away from the natural connection to our authentic self. Anything that feels like an external need is a big sign we're disconnected.

So you'd think my mirror-work experience would end there, but not quite!

Fast-forward to a short while ago, when a girl came running up to me after a workshop. She was an absolutely adorable, beautiful young thing. 'Mary, how can I meet my perfect soulmate?' she cried. 'I'm desperate!'

I laughed and said, 'Simple, my dear: just look in the mirror!'

She laughed too and said, 'No, really Mary: I've done everything and I still haven't found anyone!'

Another woman standing nearby joined in: 'What do you mean by *everything*?' she asked. The girl said: 'Well, I've done the self-love thing, trusting yourself, making space for him in my home; I've written the list, I've done the vision board…'

'My goodness, you must be exhausted!' I remarked. 'Good job you haven't met a man yet – with that amount of running around you'll probably fall asleep mid-sex!' The girl laughed and said, 'Mary, seriously: I'm really desperate!'

After wrapping up a conversation with someone else, another woman joined the discussion: 'Well, personally, I think it's all about self-love,' she said. 'I've found that the more I love myself, the more I attract love into my life.'

'But I've *done* self-love,' the girl exclaimed, frustrated. She looked at the other woman as if to say, I came to ask Mary, not you. Turning back to me she finished by saying, 'In fact, I *completely* love myself – I'm fine on the self-love thing, believe me.'

'Really?' I asked. 'Wow, I'm impressed. I've never met anyone who has completely nailed self-love. So if you have, why are you desperate for a man?'

'Mary, haven't you been listening?' the girl cried. 'I said I love myself, but I just want a man!' Now up until that point I was enjoying teasing her, but I then turned to her in all seriousness and said, 'A very wise woman once said to me that there's no such thing as an "other".' The girl looked at me, confused. 'What she means is, this has nothing to do with "getting a guy"', I added.

Unsurprisingly, she still looked confused, so I tried a different tack: 'Imagine that men don't exist...' I began. (I've never seen such horror on another person's face!) 'Bear with me, just for a moment,' I reassured her. 'Imagine there are no men on this planet. You have no interest in a same-sex relationship, and for the purpose of this conversation that never changes. So what would you do and how would you spend your time?'

The girl was still looking baffled, and it was clear that at first her mind was drawing a blank. But then, there it was: in the moment her brain shut down, a smile slowly appeared across her face and she started to laugh. Reboot, I thought!

'What would you do with all that energy, all that time, all those obsessive thoughts running around your head?' I continued. 'What would you do *just* for yourself, knowing this was how it would be, forever? Just you, no guy; he's not coming because he doesn't exist. Where would you put your focus? What is, or where is, your love now?'

I could feel the 'yes, but...' coming, but just before it reached her mouth she let out a big sigh, as if her whole body was finally breathing out and relaxing. And that was when she really got it; you could see, just as I had, that she thought she needed a man to love her in order to feel complete: to *really* experience love. Whereas you could feel her body saying, *finally, I can now focus on loving myself!*

As we walked back into the workshop together the girl asked me: 'So, are you with anyone?' I laughed and said, 'Hell, no: unlike you I had a big mirror show me last year that I'm still massively walking the self-love path. I figure that might take me a while...'

'What would *you* do if all the men on the planet disappeared?' the girl asked me. I chuckled, leaned over and whispered: 'Start selling organic, sustainable vibrators.' And with that, we both burst out laughing.

WILD AWAKENING WISDOM

- I've learned that it's hard to really give love or love another if you're unable to receive love, or love yourself. True love can only be realized from one source, and to truly love you need to be connected to the core – the source of who you are.

- If you're disconnected from yourself, you're disconnected from love, and if you're disconnected from love, you have nothing real to offer another person – let alone yourself.

- Love is who we are – it's not something we give to one another.

- Being in a relationship should be an opportunity to grow, not a need. Our experience of love exactly mirrors our level of self-love and self-worth.

- There's no such thing as rejection; no one can reject us except ourselves.

- I've learned that everything that happens on the outside is simply a mirror to what is going on inside. We create our own reality, and our own pain.

- We are never done when it comes to the journey of self-love!

Chapter 9

Where Is the Love?

*'Your own self-realization is the greatest
service you can render the world.'*

<small>SRI RAMANA MAHARSHI</small>

Recently, after some intense periods of writing, I decided to go for a walk on the common near my house. It was great: the sun was on my face, the sky was a beautiful shade of blue, laced with white swirls of wispy clouds, and I was happy that my book was finally coming together. But as I turned to head home, I spotted something shocking playing out on the other side of the street.

A man was holding his toddler with one hand, and using the other to push a young woman, presumably the child's mother, against a tree. The woman was slight and timid-looking, and as he pushed her over and over again, she just stood there submissively, with her head bowed, in a stance that looked well practised. She didn't look up at him once, or say a word.

There was no one else around to intervene, so I started walking over to the couple, becoming angrier with every step at his aggression and her lack of response. Just before I reached them, the man started to push his finger into the woman's face; her back was right up against the tree and I could hear him reprimanding her, telling her quite loudly what he thought of her.

Well, something in me fired up, and in my full feminine Leo power I could feel my chest rising, ready to roar. But then, just for a millisecond a little voice said, *Mary, leave it: you could get hurt.* I was shocked at that thought and, banishing it as quickly as it had arrived, I confronted the man. Trying not to inflame the situation further, especially as he was holding such a small child, I said quietly: 'Can you please stop. You don't need to treat another person this way, especially the mother of your child.'

The man turned and redirected his rage towards me. He came right up to my face, as if to slap me, and snarled: 'Go away, this has nothing to do with you!' I was determined to stand my ground, and that of this woman, who hadn't moved, her head still facing the ground, completely silent.

'Go away,' he said again, with his face up against mine. Then, in a controlled, steely, heavily aggressive tone that was almost more menacing than if he had hit me, he added,— 'this is none of your business.'

'No, I won't,' I said, standing firm, my whole body knowing this was not right. 'Not until you stop.' I then went over to the woman and gently said, 'No matter what you've done or think you've done, or whatever's gone on, no one deserves to be treated this way.' Furious at my remarks, the man moved up alongside me, and with his finger in my face he shouted, 'Get away from her.'

'This is none of your business,' he repeated, with his body pressed into my side and his child hanging awkwardly from his other arm. I said: 'I'm a woman and a mother and so that *does* make it my business. I'm a parent just like you, and I know there's no way I would want my son to see me and his father like this, just as I'm sure you don't want your son growing up with memories of you treating his mother this way. Is this how you want him to be around the women in his life? Really, is this the message you want to send to your child?'

I was amazed that he'd stood there long enough to listen, and even more amazed with where my words had come from. At this point a few passers-by had gathered around us and, aware this was no longer a safe space for him, the man grabbed the woman by the arm and started to walk off, pushing her along beside him.

Still saddened by the fact that at no point did she look up, I called out to the man: 'If you continue to behave like this, I'll call the police.' He stopped, turned back towards me and while walking in my direction angrily shouted: 'Don't worry, I'll call them myself.' I didn't move as he reached the spot where I was standing. 'Find a better way, both of you, to sort this out,' I continued. 'If not for you then for your child's sake; and if I come back and see you still at this, I will call the police.'

Realizing there was no more I could do at that moment, I picked up my bags and started to walk off slowly, feeling the man's anger boring a hole in my back. As I passed his 'partner' I said in a firm voice: 'No one deserves this and if you stay with him you are teaching your son that other women should also put up with this and stay too. Is this who you want your son to be, too?'

I continued on, constantly looking over my shoulder, knowing I had no intention of disappearing until I saw that the woman was okay. I knew on some level that it was pointless, but something in me felt I should just keep an eye on her. By that time I was a few metres ahead of the couple, and they were walking slowing behind me. I started to become aware of the adrenaline, the mixed emotions and the familiarity of the anger swirling away inside me. As I turned once more to check the woman was okay, the man shouted: 'Are you going to come home with us too?'

Next thing I knew, he had run up behind me. I was wondering whether this was the moment he would physically let rip. Accepting whatever might play out next, I continued walking while half-turning to face him. The adrenaline was really pumping through my body now, but I felt strangely calm. I looked him in the eye: he still had his son on one arm and it was obvious that his anger was now solely directed towards me.

Partly frustrated by his refusal to step back from his behaviour, and partly accepting that this needed to happen, I looked at the man's son and then at him and said: 'You have a beautiful child.' And he did – the boy had gorgeous chocolatey-brown eyes, silky smooth hair and creamy cheeks: you could see he was well dressed and well cared for. 'I mean it,' I went on, 'your son is such a sweet, gorgeous child. When I look at the way you hold him and the way he's dressed, I can feel that you really love him; any man who holds his child the way you do is a man who knows how to love.'

All of a sudden I could feel the fight leave his body. Baffled, and unprepared for the direction this confrontation was taking, he said: 'I do.' So I looked back at him and said, 'And that is how I know you are better than this. You are not *that* man and you do not want to be *that* kind of father. You need to believe and find a better way to sort out your problems, for your son's sake.'

Visibly moved, he gently said: 'No, I'm not like that, and I don't want to be.'

Now walking slowly next to me, with his partner quietly following behind, he said, 'Do you know what she said to me, in front of our child? We were running late so I told her to hurry up, and she told me to eff off. What kind of a way is that to talk to your husband in front of his son? Do you think that is acceptable?'

'Of course I don't know the history between you two,' I replied, 'and to be honest, I don't need to: all I'm saying is there has to be a better way than to hit, push or shout in her face – especially as your son is watching all of this. She is a woman, a human being and the mother of your child – that alone deserves some respect. I can see you are a good man, so please teach your son and each other a better way to deal with things like this.'

'You are right,' he said, looking quite remorseful. He then held out his hand to his wife and told her he was sorry. After quietly acknowledging our exchange, I walked on ahead, shocked at what had just happened and wiped out energetically by all the different emotions it had evoked. I kept thinking about that woman, and how it had angered and upset me so much to see her that way.

And then, in that moment, I saw that *I was that woman*. As I walked through the common I recognized my father energy; I recognized myself as a child; and I realized I'm every mother, every sister, every friend and brother; I'm every woman and every man. I saw that I'm no different or no less than either of those two people I'd just met.

It was such a powerful feeling and it shook me to my core. I really got that we are everyone – that we are all the same. I found a spot to sit down among the trees, so I could connect with what I was experiencing. I really felt how all of us, underneath it all, secretly desire the same things: to be seen, heard, respected, loved and felt. In effect – to be loved.

And then I thought, what kind of world would we be living in today if we all got it: if we all saw that we are everything? If we saw that nothing around us is separate or different to us; that all any of us are asking for is simply to be seen and loved? That is the world I live for, that is the path I choose to walk, and that is the person I strive to be.

QUESTION 9:
I am

> 'Did you know that the first Matrix was designed
> to be a perfect human world, where none suffered,
> where everyone would be happy? It was a
> disaster. No one would accept the program.'
>
> AGENT SMITH – THE MATRIX

This is the last of the three 'non-Questions'; originally, the wording was 'Who am I?', but, because that question can be approached from so many different angles, and I didn't want to influence the way I answered it, I later changed it to 'I am', as I explain below.

I can't quite recall when I added this final Question to the list – some time in the last few years – but I do know why I did it: because I never want to forget how amazing I am, how amazing all of life is. I want to remember and know who I *truly* am. The question 'Who am I?' has long been one of the most powerful and talked-about themes in the mind-body-spirit world, and in life in general, and when I responded to it I went into a pre-programmed way of thinking: I am a this, I am a that. I'd write things like, I am a mother; I am sad; I am a successful x,y z.

Then I removed the 'who' from the Question and somehow that opened it up, made it more expansive; instead of thinking in quite a limited way, I started to realize I was *everything*, and therefore in some way I couldn't be labelled. I realized that I am limitless and my answers changed accordingly: *I am the earth beneath my fingers. I am more than what I see in the mirror. I am more powerful than the mind can conceive!*

Now, if I'm completely honest, a lot of the time I just write the words 'I am', over and over again. Not because I am trying to be clever, but because I've realized that this is what I feel in my body – that I am truly everything. This 'non-question' has made me realize that none of us has a clue who we *really* are, and what that *really* means; we have no idea of the 'pure' power we have, right at our fingertips. So I keep 'I am' on the list to remind me of that. My expansiveness!

Below are some of the powerful lessons and insights I've discovered or experienced on a deeper level since I started asking myself Question 9. If you have any Wild Awakenings – or 'aha' moments – as you read what follows, make a note of them, and when you start to work through the 9 Questions yourself, you can explore what came up for you.

Remember that what follows is based simply on my personal experiences and on my *present* level of awareness, which is continuously deepening, expanding and growing. So please go with what works for you, and if you want to challenge, skip, or stay open to anything that doesn't, then feel free: it's your choice.

I am whatever and whoever I want to be

> *I've learned that I'm more than my labels, and powerful beyond my wildest thought.*

As soon as we start to put labels on things, we start to limit their possibilities; in fact, we also start to limit our own possibilities, our space to be 'more than'. Without realizing it we start to live the label, behaving as if we're stuck in the system and confined to the definition of the word. We lose the ability to engage and feel alive with what's right in front of us.

I remember being at a wedding reception and as the person next to me took his seat, he read my place card and asked me: 'So who *is* this Mary Daniels?' Purposely making a slightly confused face, I leaned over to him and whispered, 'I have no idea – I've *never* met her!'

Having just heard someone call me Mary, the man looked totally confused and almost lost for words. I was hoping he'd keep going with his enquiry and that we could have fun, but instead all I could see was fear: it was as if his plan to control the conversation, by dropping into CV small talk, had been taken away from him.

And this is how the majority of us live our lives – on autopilot, trapped by our multiple labels, and merely existing on the surface of what life is really about. But I've realized that I'm whatever and whoever I want to be, which in one sense means I'm everyone and everything, and that everyone else is everyone and everything too. I'm not a name, a label: I'm nothing the human mind could possibly conjure up – and that's what makes us so powerful and what makes this world, and our lives, so bloody amazing!

Stay open and be willing to question everything

I've learned that our memory can be highly unreliable, often supporting a reality we have created and/or chosen to hold on to.

We experience and perceive our 'selves' and the world around us through filters, only seeing things as we *remember* them or would like them to be. In the process, we create and live a false reality, so it's therefore important to be open to questioning things – our memories, our beliefs and our behaviour. This is something I've experienced while writing this book, and it has tested me in a way I'll never forget.

Recently, my middle brother and I had a heart-to-heart with our foster sister. Wanting us to know the truth about what had happened when the two of us joined our foster family, she invited us over and we had an open and painfully revelatory chat. As she spoke, my brother sat quietly beside me, his still, gentle body confirming that he had either witnessed what she was talking about, or was not surprised to hear it.

Obviously I was very young at the time and have no real memories of any of this. All I remember of my very early years is feeling loved. My sister confirmed that this was the case – my brother and I were very much loved – but she said it wasn't until a little later, closer to the time my foster sister left home, that my foster parents stepped up more.

Apparently, it was my foster sister who mostly took care of me when I was younger. Under the belief that our mother favoured boys over girls, she told us how, a lot of the time, she'd have to attend to my needs before going to school. She used to wake me, wash me and change my nappy (for reasons of economy, I was wearing Terry cloth nappies: the ones that needed to be washed by hand) before dashing off to school.

At lunchtime my sister would return to prepare lunch for us before turning to my heavily soiled nappy. Sometimes, if I'd been asleep before she left for school, she would leave me in my cot next to my mum, often returning to find my nappy had not been changed. Apparently, I would scream as she gently tried to apply nappy cream to the deep sores and blisters on my skin, a result of constant exposure to my urine-soaked nappies and blankets.

Then, after cleaning herself up so she didn't smell of babies, urine or worse, she would try to get back to school in time for her afternoon lessons – she wasn't always successful on both counts. She spoke of the difficult relationship she had with her mother and the chores she was forced to do around the house.

My poor sister. As I sat opposite her that day – her body riddled with tumours originating from stomach cancer – I thought, what must she have had to swallow over the years, in order to hold on to any sense of self? The secrets she'd been forced to keep.

We can be many things in a single moment, at the same time

I've learned that we can be many things in a single moment, which is why it's only when we accept the whole of who we are that we can experience the perfect expression of life that we are – the light and the dark, the yin and the yang, heaven and hell.

Accepting that I can be many things in a single moment has been one of the most powerful realizations I've had. For a long time I would hear people say: Mary, you are so confident – you are so this, so that; and at the same time as feeling confident and on top of things in one area of my life, I would also be experiencing this deep sadness and insecurity in another.

Realizing that I can be and am many things in a single moment has been amazing. It's meant I don't have to see myself or try and label myself as one fixed thing. It's meant I can finally lift the mask of having to be 'good' – or a 'goodist' as Mr Italy would often call me, jokingly. To accept that I can have dark thoughts and still be okay, and actually happy, is amazing; to know I am *not* my thoughts or my emotions – and that what I experience on a day-to-day basis is where I am *at* in my life, *not* who I am – is incredibly freeing!

I'm a perfect, divine mess

I've learned that every day is a fresh opportunity for us to mess up. And that this is okay: it merely means we're human, we're alive, and we're a perfect, divine mess – continuously being given the opportunity to learn, grow and be!

As I said in my introduction, I'm a mess. In fact, we're all a mess and at one point or another in our lives we'll mess up more than once (in my case, quite a lot). But that's also a good thing, because once we accept it we can start to get real around where we're at; we can stop taking this game called life so seriously. We can start to learn and accept our flaws and beautiful imperfections – we can play around with what they are teaching us and notice that we're no different from each other.

In the heart of this crazy, mad mess, we are perfect. Just as a plant or a tree or anything else you look at in nature has flaws, there is also a divine perfection, an innate beauty that stops it being wrong, or ugly, or bad. All we see is how perfectly beautiful that tree or plant is. Well, we are the same: for everything in life is connected and everything in life is a reflection of ourselves,

We need to save ourselves, not the planet

I've learned that the planet doesn't need saving, we do.

I've been thinking about the following questions: What if our planet is an extension of us? What if everything we see around us is a reflection of what's going on inside us? One big Louise Hay mirror trip of society, the human race!

Our lifestyles, and our levels of unhappiness, stress, obesity; young people harming themselves; the suicide rate; the depletion of the rainforests, earthquakes, tsunamis. Our collective pain and suppression. Our toxic living: I mean, look at how we're suppressing or blocking out our emotions – filling our bodies with toxins, alcohol, drugs, caffeine, pollutants. We're depleted, tired and undernourished, pushing ourselves to extremes; we're working ridiculous hours and always expecting our body to work on reserves, sometimes running out of these and hitting burnout.

What if all these 'troubles' we are seeing playing out in our environment, with the planet, are merely a reflection of the collective pain of the human race, the collective lack of self-love, of separation from self? What if it's our responsibility – our duty, almost – to look at our own suffering. To be willing to really go there if we are going to have any hope of repairing the damage done to our planet. I'm not the first person to think this, and I certainly won't be the last.

Basically, what I'm asking is this: is it the planet that needs saving – or us? You already know where I stand on this!

WILD AWAKENING WISDOM

- I've learned that I'm powerful beyond my wildest thought; I'm everything and nothing at the same time.

- I've learned that we create our own reality based on our experiences, memories and level of awareness. And while this is unavoidable, it's important to remember our minds aren't reliable and our memories can be tainted. So we should never be afraid to challenge them, and stay open-minded.

- I've learned that I'm a perfect, divine mess, and that making mistakes, messing up from time to time and having all these crazy thoughts, are all part of this divine perfection, this crazy side of life. And it's all good!

- I've learned that I can be many things in a single moment: confident and insecure, happy and sad, lonely and surrounded by people… lots of things. And that this is normal and okay. As long as I don't get too caught up on the labels and what it all means, everything will be okay.

- I've learned that if everything is one big mirror of what's going on inside of me, if I don't address how connected I am with myself, on an emotional, energetic and physical level, that will literally play out in the external environment, the planet, and beyond!

Part III

Living Your Wild Awakening

Introduction

'I've found that stillness never lies, and it's in those quiet moments that the answers to some of my biggest questions just appear.'

Welcome to the part of the book where I show you how you can incorporate my Daily Prep, including the 9 Questions, into your own life.

So, I've laid bare my crazy life, my disastrous mistakes, and some of the ridiculous, deep and profound things that have happened to me in Parts 1 and 2 of the book; I've shared all of my most intimate stories and experiences with you, and the lessons I've learned from them. I've also given you snippets of how I answer my 9 Questions, and now it's your turn to take a deeper look at your own life.

I know many of us still believe there's a 'fast lane' to getting what we want, and in some ways we can't be blamed for it, because this way of being and living has been sold to us for so many years. And sadly, quite a lot of it has come from the get-rich-quick/naive and 'unknowing' side of the self-help/personal development world: hence my mixed feelings about working in it and being a part of it.

Anyway, while life *is* of course incredibly magical, it does require us to realize this. And to do so we need to *experience* and *connect* to the deeper meaning of what it's all about – basically, why we are here and who we really are. As my heroine Byron Katie says, 'You

Need to Do the Work!' So, if you've skipped some parts of the book, please stop cheating yourself: go back and read everything else before starting on this section.

Remember, my Wild Awakening unfolded slowly, over years, and it will continue to do so until the day I die, so there's no undiscovered formula or magic wand to life. This is about loving yourself enough to believe you're worth this exploration of self – it's about giving yourself the time and creating the space to reconnect with who you truly are. If you don't do this now, then when will you?

So, no more excuses that you're too busy; if you are really short on time you can just answer the 9 Questions in the morning: which can be done in 9 minutes! We can all find 9–10 minutes in our day, and if we can't, then as I found out the hard way, there is something seriously wrong with the way we are spending our days.

Chapter 1

Working the Daily Prep

'Wealth is the ability to fully experience life.'
Henry David Thoreau

Introducing Your 'Daily Prep'

The best way to look at your Daily Prep is to imagine it's a recipe made up of three basic ingredients – three simple actions that are done every morning to prepare you for your day, in the same way that all good restaurants 'prep' before they open their doors for service. I've found that this combination of actions (see below) is a great way to raise my awareness around how I am as a person, and it also calms my infamous monkey mind! Here are the ingredients that make up the Daily Prep:

1.   Connecting with nature

2.   Being still

3.   Asking the 9 Questions

How much time does the Daily Prep take?

I usually spend up to 40 minutes on my Prep: 10–20 minutes or so connecting with nature and being still and between nine and

18 minutes on the Questions (so, between one and two minutes on each Question). If I am in a rush, I'll do my *espresso version* of the Daily Prep (five minutes of being still, five minutes in nature and nine minutes – one minute per question – on answering the 9 Questions).

I won't lie: I do miss the odd morning, or skip parts of the Prep when I don't plan my time or my day properly; sometimes I just spend 10 minutes doing the grounding exercise below and answering the 9 Questions (I am getting much better at planning my mornings, but I'm still a student). But I do try to do the Prep every morning, to feel more connected to the day ahead.

Now, once you get into the swing of this, you can always build on your Daily Prep, and personalize it! Depending on how much time you have in the morning, you may find that reading a chapter from an inspiring book, or a poem, can help you prepare for your day, and you may decide to add these activities to the basic three ingredients above.

So, feel free to tailor or tweak the practice to suit your own tastebuds – but bear in mind that the 9 Questions should be done as early as possible in the morning, and that it's important not to remove any of the Questions or change their format/order: that would be like making chicken soup without the chicken – vegetarian chicken soup is no longer chicken soup!

Does it matter what order I do it in?

I find that connecting with nature *before* I answer the 9 Questions works best for me. If I go to the park across the road from my house, I will sometimes take my journal with me, so once I've spent some time in nature, sitting in silence, I will answer my questions as I sit among the trees, or next to the lake on a park bench.

It's up to you how you do it, although I would say it's best not to leave the 9 Questions until too late in the day, as before you know it, events are under way and the habits and lack of awareness have already kicked in. Ultimately though, it doesn't matter in what order you do the Daily Prep: just remember to do it before your day properly starts. It's also important to ground yourself before asking the 9 Questions. 'Grounding' simply means coming out of your head, connecting to your body and being present – 'earthed' for want of a better word. So, as part of my Daily Prep, here are a few ways I *ground* myself.

1. Connecting with nature

Throughout the book I've talked a lot about how I've come to appreciate the amazing gifts of nature – I've learned that spending time in the natural environment, really connecting with it, is very powerful, costs nothing and can be experienced almost anywhere. I find that doing this helps me step back and put things into perspective before I answer the Questions. It also gives me a great sense of being alive. Here's an exercise I love to do as part of the grounding aspect of my Prep.

Exercise: Walking barefoot on grass or earth

This is amazing – it makes you feel held and balanced. It's so simple and you can do it in your garden, if you have one, or in any bit of green space near your home. If you have neither of these things, just do it outside, anywhere. If you are stuck indoors, do it on the floor, imagining you are outside on some grass:

- First kick off your shoes, and then head outside and either walk or stand barefoot on the ground – feeling the soft grass under your feet.

- As you do this, imagine that you're breathing in all the great energy that the Earth holds; hold it in your body and then slowly breathe out.

- If you're feeling stressed, imagine that all of your worries and concerns are just draining out of the soles of your feet: Mother Earth can handle it, she's a great recycler!

Hugging a tree

I'm serious about this one! I find that hugging a tree produces an amazing feeling – very calming, soothing and healing! I remember the first time I did it *properly* – as in embracing the tree with my heart, square on, breathing in all of the energy Mother Nature has to give us. It was so funny.

One day, while I was walking alongside my local park, my whole body started saying, over and over: *You need to hug a tree!* In the end I gave in to the urge, and looked around for a suitable candidate. Suddenly I saw a tree that just 'spoke' to me: the poor thing was naked, without leaves, its branches having recently been chopped off. Feeling a bit self-conscious, I went over and patted it, and it seemed to laugh back at me, as if to say, *Is that the best you can do?*

I then walked around the tree a few times, trying not to get my feet too close to its base, for fear of rubbing up against all the dog pee. Finally, I put my hands on the tree's trunk and just stood there, feeling it smile back at me. Super-conscious that I was being watched by people sitting in stationary cars, I then decided to take the cool approach to tree-hugging – I turned my back on my subject, pretending I was just leaning on it, and slowly slid my arms around its girth.

Now I'm sure the people watching were thinking, *Just hug the damn tree already*; either that or they were baffled by this woman who looked as if she was about to make out with a tree. Anyway, to cut a long story short, I finally gave the tree a big, full-on heart hug and a kiss. Unfortunately, my chosen specimen was riddled with bugs and angry ants, which started to crawl down my arms and into my hair – prompting me to run off screaming, and shaking my hair like a crazy woman. I've since got better at this form of connecting with nature!

2. Being still

I've found that it's in the still, quiet moments in my life that the answers to some of my biggest questions just arrive – downloaded or absorbed from the Cosmic Google. So as part of my Daily Prep I create a few moments of stillness at the start of the day, giving myself the chance for quiet reflection before I answer the Questions. I find that deep breathing is a good way of doing this (see below). And later, as I go about my day, whatever that might look like, I look for other opportunities to just Be Still.

Deep breathing

Spending even a couple of minutes or so doing some deep breathing is a great way of bringing myself into the present moment. Sometimes I do it with my eyes closed; at other times I keep them open – either way, I just follow my breath as much as I can. As I explained earlier in the book, I'll also occasionally do a more traditional form of meditation that involves deep breathing, but I won't lie about my competence in this – I'm still a long way from being able to call it a real part of my practice.

Staring at the ceiling

This is a strange one, but I've found that just lying on my back on my bed – completely awake – and staring up at the ceiling is really powerful. Usually I'll spend a few minutes doing this as part of my Prep, but I've been known to spend the whole day doing it – not moving or speaking or even eating, just lying there. I find it really calms me: it's as if my thoughts run out of steam and every part of my body is allowed to relax. I imagine my worries and my thoughts running out of every cell in my body and falling away. It brings me such clarity and peace – as if in that moment nothing else matters.

A dear friend and colleague once said that you can tell something big is about to happen when Mary spends *the day* lying on her bed – and was always right! Some might call this a form of meditation, but I'm not sure I would go that far; I'm just happy to stick with calling it being still!

Cloud-watching

I love lying on the grass, especially on my local common, and just looking up at the sky. As I listen to the sounds around me, I watch the clouds. I imagine I'm a cloud, looking down on myself and all the other humans in the world; watching us all rushing around like crazy: but for what?

Being present

Regardless of how I find stillness, I believe it's really all about being present – allowing as much distraction to flood out of my body as possible, or observing it but not getting caught up in it. I've noticed that I struggle with this sometimes because my mind is so full of chatter (those monkeys again!), so I use the following two-part technique to bring myself back to the present moment. I've found it allows me not just to connect with nature, but also to actually *experience* the beauty of nature. Here's how it's done.

Exercise: Presence through the senses

- When you're next sitting out in the garden, or in the park, or in any green space, imagine that you're from a different planet and have never seen the trees, plants, grass and other natural things in your vicinity. Or imagine you've had all your senses taken away and one by one they are being restored – so this is the first time you've ever used sight, sound, smell and touch.

- As you look around you from this new perspective, ask yourself *What do I see?* Try to *experience* what you see, rather than just describing it with words. First, *experience* what you see through *sight* – so just sit and see, literally *feel* sight.

- Then ask yourself: *What do I feel?* and again, without using words, try to experience what you *feel*. Next ask yourself: *What can I hear?* Again, experience what you *hear*: just sit and listen.

- Finally, ask: *What can I smell?* Experience what you can *smell* – even if you can't smell anything, experience what 'nothing' smells like. So the whole exercise is a total sensory experience (sight, hearing, touch and smell).

- For the next part of the exercise, try to imagine what it feels like to be a flower, a blade of grass or a tree. If you can, try to touch one of these things, and imagine you're an extension of it. For example, with your hand on the side of a tree trunk, imagine that you are that tree: standing tall and looking out across the landscape.

- Imagine your roots, deep inside the ground, held stable and steady; feel your roots. Feel your leaves and branches, and all the birds, squirrels, spiders, ants, everything, climbing up and down you, nesting in you. This exercise always makes me feel so connected and so, so peaceful and still. (If you are bug phobic, introduce it slowly!)

Meditation

And finally, let's not forget good old meditation! My plan is to actually get my backside to a Vipassana very soon – 10 days of silent meditation. So I do meditate, as best I can, but it is still a work in progress. If you get into meditation *properly*, it is very powerful. It's a great way to help still the mind, slow things down and really reconnect. Meditation is the Holy Grail of stillness!

What if the weather is bad, or I've no green areas near my home?

There are still plenty of things you can do if the weather is bad, as not every part of the Prep needs to be done outdoors. If you want to connect to nature from indoors, get yourself some great plants and do some of the exercises while you're sat alongside them. Or you can pull up a chair next to a window or a glass door leading onto the garden, and just look out on nature – you can still see the trees and watch the clouds! If it's raining, I still go outside – sometimes in flip flops – so I can stand barefoot and then easily come in and wash my feet. Earth is earth, even when it's wet! So there's plenty to work with and you can get creative with your own ideas.

3. Asking the 9 Questions

Let's now take a look at how to ask and answer the 9 Questions. But first, here's a reminder of what they are:

1. What have I learned about myself?

2. What do I accept?

3. What do I need to let go of?

4. What am I truly, deeply grateful for?

5. What do I really want to invite into my life?

6. What is my intention, and why?

7. I trust

8. I love

9. I am

As I mentioned earlier, it's important to ground yourself before you start to ask yourself the 9 Questions – to avoid it becoming a very 'heady' process – and being still and connecting to nature are great ways to do this. However, if you are really pushed for time – i.e. you only have 10 minutes or so in total – or you want another option with which to ground yourself, or you find you suddenly start moving back into your head and start overthinking the Questions, then the exercise below can keep you connected throughout the process!

Exercise: Writing from the heart

- Find yourself a comfortable chair, in a place where you won't be disturbed. Sit with your back straight, feet flat on the floor (ideally without shoes). Close your eyes and then start to imagine that you're stepping back from the craziness of life and reconnecting to the ground beneath your feet. If you're feeling tense, you can rotate your shoulders a few times, lifting them up and rolling them backwards, before allowing them to sink downwards towards the Earth.

- Then, keeping your back straight and head upright, imagine that you are working your way down/through your body internally – as if every organ, every part, is being pulled by gravity, down towards the Earth. Allow all the stress, tension and worry from that part of your body to drain out of you.

- Then take some deep breaths, making sure your shoulders don't lift up as you do so, and imagine you're breathing in through the soles of your feet – as if you're outside and they are snuggled into the soft brown earth.

- Keeping your eyes closed and shoulders relaxed, continue to breathe deeply. Now imagine that you're drawing in the amazing life energy below your feet – that beautiful sea of rich buzzing energy that feeds the plants and sustains all life forms. Imagine this same energy is flowing through every cell in your body as you continue to breathe deeply.

- Once you've done this a few times, move your focus to your heart. Place your hand on your heart and imagine it opening up, so you are breathing through your heart chakra (as we hippies call it!) Then start to take long, deep breaths, in through your heart – breathing in for a count of three and then out for a count of three.

- When the time feels right, you can begin to ask yourself the 9 Questions. If you wish, you can keep your hand on your heart as you do so. Keep breathing deeply to remind yourself to stay connected to your body and not overthink your answers.

Recording your answers

I use a journal to record my answers to the Questions, as writing things out by hand is by far the more powerful way of connecting to ourselves. As you ask each Question, try to *feel* the answer in your body before you write it down. Just go with what comes up naturally for you: without censorship, without trying to work out the meaning or the sense of it; pure and simple freestyling! I've given some examples of how I answer each Question in the relevant chapters in Part II, and below you'll find some more from two of my coaching clients.

As I mentioned above, I like to spend up to 18 minutes writing down my responses (two minutes per Question), but I've found that I still enjoy great benefits (and often experience many realizations) when I have less time. So, around 18 minutes is ideal, but the exercise is still very powerful even if you only spend a minute on each Question (nine minutes in total).

I must stress that it's really important not to judge yourself as you answer the Questions: although you're observing your behaviour, remember that nothing is fixed – what you observe doesn't define you, or label you. As I've said before, we can be *many* things in a single moment – we can be really angry and frustrated at someone and love them at the same time – so I invite you to let go of any fixed thoughts or beliefs around what your answers *should* be, and just share honest insights with yourself.

The main challenge I had when I first started answering Question 1 – 'What have I learned about myself?' – was staying in a neutral place and observing rather than judging. This was pretty difficult for me, as I'm naturally quite critical of myself. Self-enquiry is supposed to be a liberating process, one that allows us to see how we're creating the life we're living; allowing us to see our habits and our thought- and decision-making processes. What it isn't supposed to be is an excuse to pick ourselves apart.

So please join me in being kind and loving to yourself, as well as coming from a neutral and honest place. (In some ways, it's good to answer the Questions as if you're looking at yourself through the eyes of a Martian: simply observing and noting the findings!) So, go grab your journal and dive in! Have fun, relax and remember: this is your personal time – for and with yourself; it's your time to prepare the internal, so over the course of the day, you can experience a great external!

9 Questions case studies

In my time as a life coach, I set several of my clients a 28-day Daily Prep challenge and they had good results with it. Below are extracts from two of these: in sharing them I hope you'll see the kinds of things that come out of the practice.

My first client, Kevin, did his challenge in 2013, just before I changed from seven questions to eight and then nine! Since then, he has continued to send me updates on a regular basis, and has realized his dream of changing careers: he has qualified as a hypnotherapist and now has his own practice called New Dawn (how cool is that!)

1. **I've learned** *that being a better version of me on a daily basis is ample evidence of what I'm trying to achieve personally. I've learned it's imperative*

that I review each night what I've done: to celebrate what was good and acknowledge what could be improved. It's a basic 'debrief' that doesn't take too long.

2. **I accept** that I don't always do the above: that I don't always make the time to take part in an activity that's clearly for my benefit. Therefore, this is an area for development, not self-attack.

3. **I let go** of expectations that leave me feeling flat and focusing on the lack. Instead, I choose to magnify the good!

4. **I'm truly, deeply grateful** for all the lessons I've received so far: those that teach me about myself; those that are really testing; those that show me how to walk my talk, and how to be consistent in my approach.

5. **I invite** clarity in knowing what's serving me for a greater purpose, and what isn't.

6. **I intend** to play full-out; to clear away the clutter of what is me in survival mode, and focus on what it is that serves me. Also, development of self and others – intake of workshops/talks on a weekly basis. Music – seek out new talent/adding people on social network who share the same passions. Travel – commit to booking places, without fear of losing revenue/income. Food – try one new recipe a week. I feel the need to share and pursue all of these passions.

7. **I love** others' enthusiasm for life when they realize their own purpose, and how inspiring that is to everyone who comes into contact with them. I love that my presence has a calming effect on people; that more times than not, kindness, warmth and compassion are reflected back to me in my interactions with others.

In January 2015, Kevin sent me an update on a few of the Questions:

1. **I've learned** that there's a great deal of communication in stillness. That it's imperative that I practise meditation and do my Daily Prep. There is no doubt in my mind that I need to do some space-clearing prior to starting my day.

2. ***I accept*** that I won't always have all the answers, and that sometimes I'll fail to the point of feeling disappointed. However, I know there's always a lesson for me in this, and that it's all temporary. I accept that patience and persistence are key to my success.

3. ***I let go*** of the preoccupations of my 'lack lists', and instead focus on gratitude for 'what is'. I let go of impatience, laziness, comfort eating and self-doubt, recognizing that these are all low-frequency thought processes that keep me content, but don't take me to another level of contentment.

4. ***I trust*** that my consistent efforts will reap rewards far beyond my expectations. That in remaining true to my core and listening to my inner being, I'll come up with proper assessments, and therefore decisions, around which thought to choose.

5. ***I love*** that I can create my thoughts and desires so specifically and genuinely. I love the experiences I'm having now, the growth this promotes in me, and the ability to change direction at any time. I love everybody in both my immediate and distant circles, for they all have given me something. I'm creating contentment, love, happiness and joy in myself and in others.

Here's another response to the challenge, from Nicky. The first part of the list was created at the beginning of the process, when Nicky found herself thinking instead of really feeling the answers; the second part is at the end – after I showed her the 'Writing from the heart' exercise. At the time, Nicky's relationship with her partner was breaking down.

Day 2

1. ***I've learned*** that I have my role to play.

2. ***I accept*** that I need to learn and grow from this.

3. ***I let go*** of constantly blaming myself.

4. ***I'm truly, deeply grateful*** for the door that has opened for a new place to live.

5. *I invite* more lessons to be learned from this.

6. *I intend* to grow and evolve rather than shrink and dissolve.

7. *I trust* that I will be okay.

8. *I love* that I was honest and voiced my feelings this morning.

9. *I am* manifesting a higher perspective on this painful situation, but it's difficult to keep it constant.

Day 28

1. *I've learned* that this was a relationship that showed me my inner strength – I've never realized I have this before, because of my doubts. It shows me that sometimes, breaking down is waking up. I've learned that this happened to me.

2. *I accept* that I do have areas to work on in my life – for example, my fear of being abandoned when in intimate relationships and the jealousy that can result. I accept my awareness of them and that working on them will be positive.

3. *I let go* of my previous habit of repressing these parts of myself. I'm working on these areas now and making positive steps, however small. I know the healing process has started – despite the fact that I'm nearly 40 years old!

4. *I'm truly, deeply grateful* for the pain I've felt, because it has made me stronger. I now notice myself looking forward to my future. Feeling small pockets of happiness and knowing they will increase.

5. *I invite* my life to open up more in new ways and experiences. I've already booked myself onto a creative retreat day for women; I've made some contacts to help build up my career and I invite all new opportunities into my life.

6. *I intend* to continue to explore my past pain and vulnerabilities. I really want to understand them more and learn how to be at peace with them. To be able to greet them, tell them I know they are there to protect me, but they no longer serve any purpose for me.

7. **I trust** myself so much more than ever before.

8. **I love** being me! No matter what difficulties I face, I know I will and can survive. This episode in my life has proved this. Looking back, I can see how I doubted myself, but not for long. My whole being reacted against and rejected what he upheld as 'heaven'. It has cost me my relationship with him, but it has strengthened my relationship with myself.

9. **I am okay** being the person I am. I know I can walk away from this relationship with my head held high. I opened up to my vulnerability to past pain, for the first time in an intimate relationship. He didn't want to share this with me, but I know the right person will want to. I am okay now and will continue to be okay.

Afterwards, Nicky wrote to me, saying: 'Thank you so much, Mary. This has been an eye-opening experience, and it's been so healing to do it while I was going through my break-up. I am going to print out my answers for each day and read them over.'

Incorporating elements of the Daily Prep into your day

Once I've completed my Daily Prep in the morning – specifically my 9 Questions – I try to create opportunities to incorporate elements of it into the rest of my day.

- Instead of jumping on the bus to get to the station, I'll walk there through the park – as slowly as I can, often with my shoes off. Or, during my lunch break, I'll head for the nearest bit of greenery and have a wander.

- I take a lunch break or a mid-afternoon break and do the barefoot grounding exercise (above) outdoors – ideally somewhere green.

- I will think about the intention I set for myself that morning – whether I'm still connected to it or have actually done it. Or I'll pay close attention to the way I am behaving that day, and my thoughts – observing myself around others, whether I am slowing down and really being present to the way my day is unfolding.

- I take a mini-meditation break: I simply sit at my desk and meditate for 5–10 minutes. If I'm really busy, I'll just do it while I'm in the bathroom!

- I 'fake' my nature. Nowadays you can buy some amazing recordings of nature – particularly the sounds of the ocean. I will put one of these on, and just sit and listen to it for 10 minutes, breathing slowly and just coming back into my body. This is also a great exercise to do in the morning, if the weather is really bad and you want to feel that connection to nature!

- Sometimes I will do some Louise Hay mirror work while I'm washing my hands after going to the loo! I will look at myself in the bathroom mirror and tell myself how much I love myself (even if I just say the words in my head!)

- When making decisions, I will tune in to my body and make sure I am saying 'yes' to things with my intuitive voice – making sure my whole body is in agreement and not just doing so in order to keep someone else happy.

- If I'm seeing a friend, I will ask them to meet me in the park, or along the river, and we'll go for a walk together!

- I hold a lot of my coaching sessions outside, in parks. I call these walk and talks, and clients love them! So why not have some of your work meetings outside?

There are lots of ways you can get creative with this, and over the course of the day keep plugging in and staying connected! Please, if you come up with some great ideas, let me know. Share them on my blog/site www.marydaniels.co.uk – you can never have too many ideas.

In the end, this is about a lifestyle change – a way of being rather than another chore to add to the endless list of to-dos. I am still working on my Daily Prep, but I've found that making it creative, meaningful, doable, sustainable and fun is essential! (I am even typing this chapter while sitting on a bench in the park!)

Remember: ultimately, the bigger question is *How are you setting yourself up for your day?* If you are not able to give yourself proper space to connect in the morning, not even 18 minutes to answer the 9 Questions, then you really need to ask yourself: *How important is my wellbeing?* I've had that chat with myself *many times*, and still am – it goes back to the big old self-love thing!

Chapter 2

Tools to Support Your Journey

'As a single footstep will not make a path, so a single thought will not make a pathway in the mind. To make a deep mental path, we must think over and over the kind of thoughts we wish to dominate our lives.'

HENRY DAVID THOREAU

As part of my Wild Awakening journey, I've drawn on several techniques, processes and exercises to help me in completing my Daily Prep, with the 9 Questions, and with life in general. I've shared some of these with you here, sometimes in the form of personal stories, in the hope that they might help you as you undertake your journey.

My 'very British' positive affirmations

In Chapter 9, I told you how I'd once tried Louise Hay's mirror work, and positive affirmations. As I explained, at first I struggled with these forms of self-love, unable to connect with anything I was saying or doing. I needed a gentler lead-in to self-acceptance and self-love; in fact, I almost needed to trick myself into loving myself more.

My personality has recently been described as being very 'American', which made me laugh, but back then, rather than taking the upfront, direct approach to 'loving myself' favoured by our American cousins – standing in front of the mirror and eventually coming to believe I was awesome, amazing: the best thing since sliced bread – I took what I call the British route instead, a more modest, conservative one, and started doing my 'very British' positive affirmations (all very tongue in cheek, of course).

At the time I was going through a very low period in my long-term relationship, and I knew I really needed to build up my self-confidence and self-belief. So I'd make statements in my journal about how much I liked myself, and now and then I would test out the word 'love'; I'd say things like: 'I love the way you found that lovely apartment' after I'd found a new home for myself and my son.

Or I'd write about how I loved the meal I'd cooked, how I liked my smile, my sense of humour. I noticed that for affirmations related to my body, I could only manage to use the word 'like', but for anything connected to my son or people I cared for, I could reach 'love'. For several months I'd write these affirmations, over and over again, many along these lines:

- You are beautiful and sexy.

- You are so intelligent and good with words.

- You have a big heart and your energy radiates everywhere you go.

- You are perfect just the way you are.

- I like your curvy African figure.

Then one day I noticed that the wording had moved from being a bit timid, to sounding almost South American in tone: warm, friendly and genuinely happy with life – for example, I *love* your curvy, full figure! Eventually, I found the affirmations worked really well: I started to really like myself and people began to comment on how great I looked!

EFT – Emotional Freedom Technique

I've also found that EFT has helped me in many ways – especially around self-acceptance. Essentially, EFT is like acupuncture or acupressure, and involves tapping on specific meridian points on the body. It's designed to help with trauma and buried emotions that are not supporting us – freeing up energy blocks and stresses in our body, and helping to keep things flowing. It actually allows us to reconnect. It's a really powerful, gentle and loving way of helping us accept ourselves, and eliminating negative charges around past events.

What I really like about EFT is what's called the 'set-up phrase', where before you start tapping on the points, you tune in to the area of stress or concern you want to tap around. So I would think of something I was feeling about my body – some negative judgment I felt was true but also knew was causing me harm – and my set-up phrase was: *Even though* (my words inserted: I hate the way I look without my clothes on), *I deeply and completely love and accept myself.*

Of course, the set-up phrase varies from person to person: when I was on my EFT course, some of the people who were struggling with self-love or self-acceptance had slightly less 'in your face' phrases than mine, but I quite liked this. I believed that saying my set-up phrase over and over again would be good for me, and it was.

There is so much information on EFT online – in particular Gary Craig. Also, Karl Dawson does great work around Matrix re-imprinting, another meridian-tapping technique, which takes EFT one step further. If you search online for either of these terms, you'll find lots of information.

Byron Katie's The Work

I love Byron Katie's book *The Work* – the title alone shows you it isn't a '7 quick steps to hop, skip and jump through life'. And, having met Katie a few times – when we hosted her at Alternatives – I have to say she really appears to walk her talk; I've also had some of the nicest 'green room' chats with her in my time working there.

The Work contains the phenomenal process that Katie has created. As part of this, several worksheets take the reader step by step through a self-enquiry process that really allows us to see how we create our own pain and suffering. And then it shows us how to turn it around into something powerful – to see it for what it is (usually an illusion or a story in our heads that we've invented). Everything you need in order to do *The Work* is free to download from her website (www.thework.com).

Body talk

After a situation or an event has passed, it ceases to exist: it's over, in the past. So if it is all behind us, how is it that its energetic charge can still be triggered? What is keeping it alive? Is it being held in our bodies – the memory of it in our cells and tissues as a form of stress? Is it turning into a dis-ease or an event our mind can't let go of: a memory that is constantly being triggered?

Louise Hay's book *Heal Your Mind, Heal Your Body* beautifully reveals how every physical symptom is connected to an emotional cause. The book was a great help for me when my body started to release things while I was doing my 9 Questions, and I couldn't work out what was going on. At one time, I was vomiting and had an upset tummy, so I looked up the emotional causes of this in Louise's book, and learned they were linked to negative emotions. The book also offers positive affirmations and releasing statements that I've now integrated into my personal EFT sessions.

There are lots of great books on the market about Meta Medicine, the mind-body connection; in particular I love Bruce Lipton's ground-breaking and brilliant book *The Biology of Belief*, in which he states that our genes and DNA do not control our biology, and that instead, DNA is controlled by our environment, by signals outside the cell – our positive and negative thoughts!

I went to a couple of great workshops by Energy Medicine practitioner Donna Eden, who teaches people how to work with the body's energy systems to reclaim their health and natural vitality. She has written a fab book called *Energy Medicine* – it's like a bible! I also love Caroline Myss's work, especially her book *Anatomy of the Spirit*; she's a phenomenal woman and a font of knowledge. I could keep going: there is a lot out there!

Stepping back from our emotions

There's something else that can get in the way of my ability to observe myself properly – and that's my darn emotions! In the USA, when the police arrest someone they issue a caution that begins: 'You have the right to remain silent. Anything you say can and will be used against you in a court of law.' Well, that's exactly what I feel should be said to me when I get overly emotional!

When it comes to my 'emotional mouth', I think there should be a law to make me shut it, especially when I'm tired! Mr Italy always used to say to me: 'Why do you swallow your anger? You need to let it out!' Well, I think there have been a couple of occasions when he's regretted encouraging me to do this! If you really think about it, most of our emotional ups and downs are due to a belief, thought, or form of attachment – that we're losing something or *have* already. (Adyashanti's book *Falling into Grace* is a great introduction to this.)

Our emotions are great teachers and hold so many powerful messages and insights, but it's only when we're able to step back and observe them, rather than getting lost in them, that we can benefit from the real juiciness that's held in that space.

Techniques for holding emotions in check

When I'm going through a bit of an emotional rollercoaster, I've found that the following *physical activities* have helped me a lot. (These are much better than my previous habit of either disconnecting from my emotions, ignoring them or suppressing them by overeating or watching loads of TV and movies.)

Deep breathing

This is an obvious one that's so simple when I am emotional – I just need to remember to do it! Really grounding, deep breathing can work wonders. Just imagining with each breath that my emotions are calming down: breathing them out or letting them run into the ground.

Gardening

I love permaculture, and growing my own food. It's very relaxing and grounding: it helps me connect, come out of my mind and into my body and the moment! I used to think gardening was for elderly people – something you did when you retired. But seriously, this city girl is loving it – and it's becoming quite trendy nowadays to 'grow your own food'. I suggest joining a community scheme, or volunteering at a permaculture centre. Google The Permaculture Association (www.permaculture.org.uk) for a list of places to volunteer!

Exercise/movement

This is a great way for me to calm my emotions and step back from them: even if it's a simple walk around my local common for 20–30 minutes, connecting to nature. It allows me to think rationally and get rid of some of that frothy energy.

Listening to music and dancing

For me, this is a powerful state-changer. Whatever I'm going through or experiencing, and wherever I am, I will put on some music and dance to it. I remember once in the Alternatives office we were all feeling a little bit down, so I put on some music and got the girls up and dancing; it was fun, and exactly what we needed to dust off the emotional cobwebs! I've observed that I do tend to wallow in my emotions sometimes, and can go into a self-induced depression by listening to the most melancholy music I can find.

I actually enjoy this on occasion, but I do try to ensure that a) I don't get *too* lost in it; b) it doesn't turn into an Oscar-winning performance of emotional release; and c) I don't send any SMSs or emails while in this place! (I am still working on the last one!)

Exercise: Post-it® note your emotions

- On one large or two small post-it notes, write down all the things that have upset or angered you, and a description of all your emotions around them (this works, if you keep your handwriting small!) I've also found that if I record what I'm feeling in my journal first, I sometimes have a lot less to write on the post-it notes, as much of the emotional charge has already dissipated and I can start to see things more clearly.

- Stick your post-it notes on any door in your home (I use my wardrobe door).

- Then, as you stand in front of the notes on the door, take a big step backwards – away from them. This symbolizes your taking a step back from your emotions. Then, just take a few deep breaths and imagine that the problem/emotion written on the notes is no longer within you, but 'over there'.

- As you take a few more steps back, imagine that you're putting more distance between yourself and your emotions. Now, depending on how strong the emotions are, you'll sometimes need to take quite a few steps back before you calm down (on the odd occasion I thought I'd need an airport runway!)

- Now, on a new post-it note, write down what you think is *behind* all these emotions. What is this really all about? Tell yourself that these emotions are just messages, here to teach you something about yourself. Ask yourself: *What is the lesson or thing I'm supposed to see or get? What is the **true** feeling here; what am I unconsciously attached to? What is the fear or frustration: rejection, abandonment, being on my own, not being heard, not feeling loved?* You will get there.

- Allow yourself as long as you need to 'get' what these emotions are telling you. For me, this can usually take a few minutes, but occasionally I've had to leave the post-it notes on the door for a few days.

Now it's really important we remember to do this exercise as observers: looking at what our emotions are teaching us about ourselves, for as soon as we get into the 'he said, she said, blame thing', we're again moving away from the truth of what's really going on.

I've found that understanding this is critical to being able to resolve it properly. For me, behind every emotion is the same thing – it always, on some level, comes down to some form of attachment, or more accurately, a lack of self-love; a separation from who I truly am. Yes, I know, good old self-love again – argh, you've got to love it!

Just say 'So What?'

This is a really short and simple technique I use when I've done all I can to rectify or sort out a situation, or when I'm worried that something I've done won't be accepted, and might upset someone. I also use it when I've done something really stupid, something I regret and can't change. Basically, it helps my over-worrying, people-pleasing tendencies. Seriously, this technique is so simple and easy but so liberating for me!

It consists of asking myself two words: so what? **So what** if my email peed someone off? **So what** if they can't see where I'm coming from? **So what** if they don't like me? **So what** if I don't like them? There is only so much anyone can do, and sometimes what's done is done, so if I know I've done all I can, taken on board the lesson I need to learn and basically accepted responsibility for my part, the rest just has to come down to a simple **so what?** What's done is done.

A friend to journey with you

There isn't room here to share all of the practical exercises and techniques that have helped me during my Wild Awakening journey, so I've gone into more depth on my website/blog – www.marydaniels.co.uk, where I've created a section called 'Living your Wild Awakening'; there, in future, I'll also include space for others to share their own insights and Wild Awakenings. Remember: we are all students and teachers at the same time.

Also, if you sign up for my 'Wild Awakening offerings' newsletter on the website, you'll find further resources there. In time, I will also create some vlogs and try and mix a few things up in my blog.

So, however you piece together your own Daily Prep, try to do it as consciously as you can: be there, know yourself and your needs, and make sure you find your own natural way to enjoy it. What I will say, though, is that consciousness cannot be taught: it can only be experienced. I've found that the only way I can raise my consciousness is to raise my self-awareness – observing myself and my chosen way of being. This is something the 9 Questions have really helped with.

Of course, no matter how many times I do my Daily Prep, I will always have blind spots. However, I've learned I needn't worry about those too much. If I need to learn or see something about myself, life will always make sure it happens – often sending the lesson in the form of an experience, a loved one or a family member who'll show me exactly what I need to learn! This usually drives me crazy at first, setting off my triggers left, right and centre, but very soon I calm down and remember that I programmed this into my choices of what I wanted to experience in this lifetime! ;-)

Forever Young

Recently, while I was working in the café in my local park, I witnessed a really sweet and funny exchange between an elderly couple. They had been sitting outside having lunch and just as they were ready to leave the wife turned to her husband and asked, 'Do you want to use the bathroom before we go, dear?'

Nodding his head, he got up and went inside the café. Five minutes later, he came back out again, carrying an ice-cream. Licking it like a little boy, he walked up to his wife and said: 'Darling, can you hold this while I go to the loo?'

His wife looked slightly frustrated and asked: 'Why didn't you go to the toilet *before* you bought the ice-cream?' The man smiled and said: 'All I want you to do is hold my ice-cream, love: I'll only be five minutes.'

The wife held out her hand to take the ice-cream, and then stared at it as if it were going to attack her, 'What do I do if it starts to melt?' she asked, plaintively. As he headed off to the loo, the man called back: 'You remember what to do, dear – it hasn't been that long. Just lick it. It's a raspberry ripple – your favourite!'

Under her breath, the woman muttered: 'I don't like ice-cream, and I didn't want an ice-cream.' I continued to type away, and a couple of minutes later, out of the corner of my eye, I saw the woman enthusiastically licking away at the ice-cream cone. It made me laugh. Unaware that her husband had returned she suddenly looked up, like a little girl with ice-cream covering her top lip. She smiled, pulled out a handkerchief and wiped her mouth.

'For someone who didn't want an ice-cream you have done very well!' the husband remarked. The woman handed the cone back, and as they got ready to leave once more, he said: 'See – I knew you'd remember what to do.' I quietly laughed to myself, thinking, how sweet. And on the way home, I bought myself an ice-cream cone.

I've realized that I don't want to let go of being a child; in some ways I don't want to become 'a grown-up'. The problem with thinking we are all grown-up is that we stop learning – we close down and forget what it's like to live in wonder, open to every moment and what that brings us. Yes, living that way would mean we're a bit of a disaster at times, and we may get messy every now and then, needing someone to pick us up and clean us off, but I would rather that than not be able to feel what it means to be alive.

I wrote a lot of this book while sitting in my local park, surrounded by nature and also by young children. While my direct parenting days are over, I love children, and every now and then I would be mesmerized by them as I watched them play. I am in awe of the way they engage with life and the world around them – as if every moment is an unfolding miracle.

I once saw a little boy, maybe 18 months old, playing in a tiny puddle. He'd tentatively step into it, laugh and pull his foot out again; then sidestep around it, tiptoe up to it, and step into it again, laughing away and totally engaged with this puddle, over and over again. And while that warmed my heart, what I found even more inspiring was the way his father patiently stood there – amused by his son's antics, and watching the world through his eyes; it was refreshing and I actually found both of them adorable.

What I'm saying here is that we need to be careful that we don't start to fall into the trap of believing that all our growing is done; that being an adult is only about being responsible – getting and maintaining a job, accepting the burdens that come with paying bills, maintaining the lifestyle and wearing the social mask of niceties we all do so well.

The truth is that we never finish growing up, and our younger self, the child, doesn't go away. So when it comes to answering the 9 Questions, do it as the child that you are: be in awe and in wonder of your life and connect to every moment of your day as if it were multiple miracles unfolding right before your eyes. Because it is.

One thing I know for sure is when we commit to a path of really, truly knowing ourselves, we commit to growth and in that space of growth comes awareness – a realization that we're enough, and a deeper knowing that the life that we secretly hoped for but never really thought was possible, already is.

We start to experience the true miracle of being alive: the stuff dreams are made of and more, the true elixir of life. Where true love, real love, exists – without separation, discrimination, hatred, judgment or the need to 'have more'. But hey, what do I know? I'm a mess, remember! ;-)

Resources

Helplines

If you have been affected by any of the themes touched upon in this book, or have suffered from any form of sexual, physical or emotional abuse and could benefit from additional support, please feel free to contact a member of our team via our website (www.marydaniels.co.uk). Alternatively, listed below are some of the National Helplines that aim to provide support for those in distress.

In the UK
Samaritans:
www.samaritans.org or 08457 90 90 90

If you are at all concerned about the welfare of a young person, please don't hesitate to contact one of the organizations below:

National Society for the Prevention of Cruelty to Children:
www.nspcc.org.uk
Help for adults concerned about a child: 0808 800 5000

Childline (help for children and young people):
www.childline.org.uk or 0800 1111

In the USA
National Child Abuse Hotline:
www.childhelp.org/hotline or 1-800-4-A-CHILD (1-800-422-4453)

The Samaritans USA:
www.samaritansusa.org or 1 (800) 273-TALK

Connect with me

Sign up to our growing community of people who are interested in waking up and connecting, and enjoy more Wild Awakening Wisdom, funny stories and Keeping-It-Real exercises to help you on your journey to self:

www.marydaniels.co.uk
www.facebook.com/marybeingmary

Mary loves...

These are just some of the places, spaces and organizations that have really helped my Wild Awakening Journey.

Hazelwood House: a magical retreat space in the heart of South Devon – www.hazelwoodhouse.com

Alternatives: the events organization inspiring hearts, minds and souls – www.alternatives.org.uk

Byron Katie's The Work: www.thework.com

Connecting to Nature/Permaculture:
The Permaculture Association – www.permaculture.org.uk
Permaculture magazine – www.permaculture.co.uk
Kevin Mascarenhas – www.naturalflow.biz
The Quadrangle Trust – www.thequadrangletrust.com

Tribewanted: www.tribewanted.com

Tribewanted Monestevole (Italy): www.monestevole.it

The One-Straw Revolution: www.onestrawrevolution.net

ABOUT THE AUTHOR

Georgio Tinenti

Mary Daniels is an inspiring speaker, a powerful storyteller, a coach and an original 'wild woman'. She has spent most of her adult life working with vulnerable people in the community – including in prisons, young offenders' units, schools, women's centres and inner-city charities – where she has put to use her natural ability to transform every challenging situation into a triumph.

The former Co-Director of Alternatives, one of the UK's longest-running Mind, Body, Spirit Organizations, Mary has also been invited to work with leading companies and charities including JP Morgan, the International Dermal Institute, Fulham Football Club, The NCS Trust and Mosaic, the charity founded in 1997 by HRH The Prince of Wales to create opportunities for young people growing up in the most deprived communities. Mary has won awards for her mentoring and coaching and has recently launched her new consultancy, which works with conscious individuals and organizations who are ready to get real about where they're at, get clear on what they want and find the courage to go do it!

No matter what Mary is involved with she hopes her quest to continue 'waking up' will inspire others to join her in courageously embracing the life they were born to live.

www.marydaniels.co.uk

HAY HOUSE

Look within

Join the conversation about latest products,
events, exclusive offers and more.

 Hay House UK

 @HayHouseUK

 @hayhouseuk

 healyourlife.com

We'd love to hear from you!

Printed in the United States
by Baker & Taylor Publisher Services